I'm Over All That

I'M OVER ALL THAT

And Other Confessions

Shirley MacLaine

ATRIA BOOKS

NEW YORK   LONDON   TORONTO   SYDNEY

ATRIA BOOKS

A Division of Simon & Schuster, Inc.
1230 Avenue of the Americas
New York, NY 10020

First Atria Books hardcover edition April 2011

ATRIA BOOKS and colophon are trademarks of Simon & Schuster, Inc.

For information about special discounts for bulk purchases, please contact Simon & Schuster Special Sales at 1-866-506-1949 or business@simonandschuster.com.

The Simon & Schuster Speakers Bureau can bring authors to your live event. For more information or to book an event contact the Simon & Schuster Speakers Bureau at 1-866-248-3049 or visit our website at www.simonspeakers.com.

Designed by Joseph Rutt/Level C

Manufactured in the United States of America

10   9   8   7   6   5   4   3   2   1

Library of Congress Cataloging-in-Publication Data

MacLaine, Shirley, 1934–
    I'm over all that : and other confessions / Shirley MacLaine.
        p.   cm.
    1. MacLaine, Shirley, 1934–   2. Entertainers—United States—Biography.
3. Spiritualists—United States—Biography.   I. Title.
    PN2287.M18A3   2011
    791.43'028'092—dc22
    [B]   2011000705

ISBN 978-1-4516-0729-1
ISBN 978-1-4516-0731-4 (ebook)

For Peter

Overture

All life, even the cruelest drama and most absurd comedy, is a form of show business, a kind of performance, and I have been lucky enough to have created the moving picture show of my own life. I have starred in it, produced it, written it, directed it—even financed and distributed it. What's even better is that I get to rerun it now and then, to see things I might have missed back then. In this third act of my life, much has become clearer. So much is over, and I am over so much.

I have learned to ease up on worry, scheming for films or roles, planning for better surroundings, and feeling anger at all our leaders who operate politically rather than humanely. Yes, I am over all that. I'm over listening to advertisements, the latest fashions (I never was much for that), events I should attend in order to be seen, red carpet madness. I'm getting more and more free from the expectations of the external world. In fact, the one worry I can't seem to give up and get over is a lingering fear that being a reclusive, happy, older woman may not be entirely healthy. But who says so? I'm not interested in parties, new outfits (only comfortable ones), being socially acceptable, and whether I'll be on anyone's so-called A-list. My goodness, what a way to live!

I'm *not* over going to the movies, seeing live theater, hearing symphonies, eating a good dinner (I'm learning to dine out alone), attending a worthy charity event (for half an hour), visiting a sick friend, or taking treats and toys to the animal shelter.

I am over what other people think (I got over that a long time ago), and trying to persuade them to come around to my point of view about anything.

One thing will always be a constant with me. I have a guiding sense of curiosity. I will never get over asking *Why*. This questioning has been with me all my life. It is my sustenance, my inspiration, my joy, and my intellectual food and color. I will never be over my search for the Big Truths. And I'm not the only one. Most people I've met around the world believe we are not alone in the universe but will not talk about this openly because they're terrified of being humiliated publicly for their beliefs. Some scientists, academics, and movers and shakers I've met were even reluctant to discuss it privately because of how they might be perceived. (Just another reason I revere the brilliant and fearless Stephen Hawking!)

Everywhere I've traveled in the world I've found that people are looking for something to fill the loneliness inside them; they are after what I think of as "The Big Truth." It doesn't matter how wealthy or well situated they are; after surface talking, joking, eating, Hollywood gossip, and cultural politeness, the conversation always turns to why are we here, what is the point of life, is God real, are we alone in the universe? That's because, like me, most people have realized that money isn't the answer to their emptiness. In fact, it sometimes contributes to it because the management of money (or the fear of not having enough) distracts them from any real examination of what is really bothering them.

So I've concluded that for us to get to the Bigger Truths, there is much for us to get over. I've had a good time exploring what I've finally gotten over and what I will never get over . . . from the ridiculous to the Big Sublime.

I'm glad I am in the third act of my life. I have loved my ride and am now appreciating relinquishing the reins and looking back. Sometimes I feel an unbearable ecstasy of loneliness for some of my past, wishing now that I had been so much more present then. Sometimes I feel it all happened to someone else, and I long to get the "me" of it all back. How could I have done so much, been so many places, known so many people—and now it is all past, gone, memories of colorful stories like little movies attached to the celluloid of my brain tissue. Every now and then the little movies turn themselves on, wanting to be rerun. What didn't I see then? What deeper meaning did I miss? Where are those actors and actresses and politicians from my past now? They are still with me, in all the things they taught me, the memories of the times we shared. Fascinating and talented people, mind-expanding conversations, and curiosity about the future—those are things I will *never* get over.

On with the show!

I'm Not Over
My Need to Know

When I look back on my seventy-six adventure-peppered years of life, I want to celebrate my "still here-ness." While I am definitely more *still* now, I do like being *here*. One of my great passions in life was traveling, which I'm sorry to say is not true anymore. *I'm over all that.* I like being here where I am. And I like being still.

The idea of walking through an airport in a state of terror over the idea that the TSAs ("Thugs Standing Around") won't let Terry, my terrier dog, on the plane with me is my worst nightmare. What has happened to us? We obediently cower in fear, hardly even made uneasy by the thing that should really scare us: our own acceptance of the foregone conclusion that the possibility of terrorism trumps our freedom to travel.

I'm over that conclusion. I don't believe that terrorism is the real reason we have become saluting robots. I believe we have neglected to see that terrorism is just a convenient excuse for those in power to gently instruct us to go quietly into that good night of being compliant and unrevolutionary citizens who willingly become subjugated to authority.

Tom Paine has always been my idol. He wrote of the common sense of starting a revolution and praised the Age of Reason instead of religion. Of course, he's buried in a potters' field somewhere where no one can pay respects. He flew too much in the face of accepted behavior, which didn't sit well with those whose first priority was political popularity and maintaining the status quo. People like that tend not to be the ones who get the big memorials and shrines dedicated to them.

The blood of the Founding Fathers runs through my veins because I was born and raised in Virginia, the real birthplace of our American Revolution. It was also the place of metaphysical leadership—the Masonic Order. But there will be time for words like "metaphysics" later. I got over the box-type religious thinking a long time ago too, because I wanted to breathe. That is what freedom is for.

I find it interesting and more than coincidental that I developed asthma during the "W" administration. I was so frustrated with his idiocy and perpetration of harm that I literally couldn't breathe. I ended up in the emergency room three times, and each time I felt what it must be like to die of asphyxiation. I felt the land of the free was becoming asphyxiated, too. People were so dumbed-down they didn't even realize they weren't in charge of their own lives or thoughts anymore. Whether 9/11 was planned by people other than Osama bin Laden and Al Qaeda, I don't know. But it certainly was conducive to the endeavor of dispensing with our individual freedom, which was supposed to be our inalienable right and the defense of which should be the primary reason we would ever go to war in the first place. We were told we should patriotically fight and kill those who would rob us of our freedoms. We didn't need Osama. We allowed it to happen by not questioning our own elected leaders who said national security should be our highest priority.

For me, the searching of my bags and the patting down of my body *and* my dog is unconstitutional. Once, in Los Angeles, a big, fat, slovenly guy made me walk back and forth with Terry (26 pounds) four times through security because my boarding pass was turned the wrong way. I found myself hissing like a cat and hating these authoritarian men who were exercising their power over me, a well-known and (admittedly) privileged woman. I heard he got fired later. Maybe he picked on Rosie O'Donnell.

Traveling for me is a constant reminder here and abroad that we are becoming afraid of ourselves and our neighbors, because *fear is the most powerful weapon of mass destruction.* I don't want to get over my abhorrence of such a condition. But I am over traveling, except when absolutely necessary, or unless a Pleiadean spacecraft offers me a ride to a planet where they claim to have solved such matters.

I hate that I'm over traveling because of all this security bullying. It was a multilayered experience for me everywhere I went before. I learned so much about myself because when

I found myself splashed up against a foreign environment, *I* was all I had and all I could depend on. I never traveled as a privileged person. I rarely even went first class. I wanted to experience the "real" world away from what had been the elitist world where I'd lived since coming to Hollywood when I was just twenty. If and when people recognized me, I followed the flow where it took me and more often than not, I made new friends.

Traveling has been my greatest teacher. It has offered me the gift of seeing and experiencing other points of view and other "realities." Ever since the early days of film, the American movie screen reached around the world and I found that wherever I went, people told me their most private secrets, I assume because I was famous and they somehow felt they knew me. They were flattered that I was interested in them and listened. I quickly learned that my American version of the truth was not necessarily anyone else's. Not only was truth relative, it was constantly changing.

I found that life itself was theater. Each culture played its own part. Sometimes the characters in my travels were mean and unethical. Sometimes they were kind and trustworthy. Sometimes events were comical, sometimes dramatic. I had been playing an American woman all my life, so when I traveled I could break out of this typecasting and feel I'd become a member of a new culture. I began to have a more objective view of myself, and my point of view of almost anything became more flexible. By the time I was forty years old, things that previously would have been morally wrong to me were now lessons, not judgments . . . even regarding death.

I remember riding along a *klong* (waterway) in Bangkok, Thailand. I could see the activities of the *klong* dwellers as I glided past on my hired canoe. Suddenly, not more than one hundred feet away, a very young baby leaned over the side of the family canoe and toppled headfirst into the water. I strained my eyes to find him. The parents heard his coughing and gurgling, turned around, but did nothing to rescue their child. He disappeared under the water and drowned. I sat stunned, wanting to go in after the child myself, but my guide stopped me. From the Buddhist point of view, one should never interfere with the karmic will of God. If the parents or anyone else had jumped in to save the child, they would have placed him in a position of obligation for the rest of his life. The child's life would have *belonged* to his rescuer. And this was one fate a Buddhist would never willingly inflict on another.

To a Buddhist, death is only another form of life anyway. Death is part of the cycles of life. Life and death are not regarded in terms of an individual's survival or loss. The fate of the drowning child was not to be interfered with. The outcome was accepted as part of God's will. By the same token, killing is abhorred because the act of killing *is* interfering with God's will. There is, to a Buddhist, a profound difference between killing and allowing a death to occur. Fate and destiny are their philosophy and religion. I remember a friend of mine who owned a private plane saying he would never have a Buddhist pilot because that pilot would be too serene in allowing a crash to happen—fate and destiny again.

A few days after witnessing the death of that child, I went to a Thai boxing match. What distinguishes Thai boxing from any other kind is that kicking anywhere and any way is legal. The boxers wore groin cups in their trunks to protect themselves, but otherwise no form of padding or protection. In a ceremony before the match, the boxers entered the ring and performed prayers and reverence to Buddha. Each boxer prayed for the well-being of his opponent, not himself. A group of musicians began to play as each boxer performed ritualistic dance movements and stylized pantomimes in benevolent reverence for the fate of his opponent. A signal was given, whereupon the boxers proceeded to kick, smash, jab, and pummel their opponent with both fists and feet. No holds were barred. One of the boxers kicked the other in the head and snapped his neck and broke it. The man died right there on the spot.

I couldn't believe that this was a popular sport for the peaceful Thai people, but the huge crowd went wild with enthusiasm. Two new boxers entered the ring and performed the ritualistic prayers and bowed to Buddha with mime and ritualistic dancing. The combat began. One sliced the other across the forehead with his elbow, causing blood to pour down his face. The roar of the crowd at the sight of blood was deafening. They shouted their approval above the ear-splitting music that was being played. A doctor was summoned, but the crowd chanted wildly, "Let him fight!" The wounded boxer stamped his foot until the doctor went away. Again the crowd roared its approval. The wounded boxer attacked his opponent, smearing his blood all over them both. His adversary continued kicking the head wound open further and further. Blood was flying everywhere. The crowd was ecstatic. I was stunned and almost apoplectic. The doctor came back and the crowd booed. Two stretchers were ordered since the head wound was completely open now. Both boxers looked more like human protoplasm than men. Finally, the match was stopped, much to the anger of the audience.

Yes, Thailand was a paradox. But aren't we all? One person's entertainment is another person's hell.

I began to speculate on whether such a popular bloodletting sport gave the Thai people an outlet for their repressed anger and submission. Was this sport a way to vent their hostility and rage (emotions that perhaps surge in all of us)? Perhaps violent sports are necessary and preferable to the alternative things we could do to each other.

In Thailand, I was once again made aware of how parochial my values were. I had learned everything I knew from the limited confines of my childhood—from my parents, from the schools I had attended, and from the neighborhood I grew up in. As a child and an adolescent growing up in the "land of the free," I had not been educated to think beyond the parameters of what my traditional teachers wanted me to know. My parents always tried to protect me from harm if I dared attempt too much. In effect, they put up a three-foot-high emotional fence around me. I learned to jump over it. They would then erect something a few feet higher. I would jump over that, too. They never made me feel afraid—they just wanted to protect me. Maybe I sought out so many dangerous adventures in my life because my parents made me see that there were a host of potentially scary things out there in the world, but didn't do so in a way that would stifle my curiosity. In effect, they were teaching me *how* to jump. That's what I've been doing all my life. Intentionally or not, my parents taught me how to jump over my own walls in life and to *dare*.

When I look back on some of my experiences, I'm intrigued by which ones I recall as being important. There seems to be a separation of heart experience and mind/body experience. If I were to write a book today just about my travels, it would result in a different book from the ones I wrote in the past. The truth is that no matter where I went, I was always looking for myself. That journey into myself as I evaluated my beliefs and values, whether living at home or in far-flung corners of the world, has been the most important journey of all. That journey is what led to my search to understand the true meaning of spirituality. I was learning that I truly was creating everything. I was attempting to understand the character I had created as myself in the theater of life.

I'm Over Being Concerned About What I Shouldn't Do

I like ageing because I can forget all about the things that mattered in the past. I used to think it really mattered if I wore high heels to a premiere or not. Can you imagine? Over the years, I've realized that the "theater" of the past is a script I no longer want to play a part in.

The older I get, the more adventurous my script becomes, maybe even risky. But there is no fun to be had in a safe script. I learned that from watching my parents. I left the safe harbors of my parents and childhood in order to sail with the wind a long time ago. I explored and explored, and always the journey took me inward.

I acknowledged the theater of war, the theater of politics in Washington, the theater of television news. . . . If we humans were writing the scripts and acting in the theaters of reality, I wanted to change my script. I decided to explore the theater of inner truth.

I'll Never Get Over Trying to Understand Men and Women (Especially on a Movie Set)

I have many actress friends around my age, and when we get together we discuss how difficult it is, and always has been, to be a woman in this movie business obsessed with youth and sexuality and beauty. We know we have had to be tough and resilient, but have we also lost our feminine vulnerability? What good is being vulnerably feminine, anyway? I don't think men really prefer that.

When I look at the pictures on my Wall of Life, the wall in my home where I've hung hundreds of photographs documenting movies and many different moments of my life journey, the faces peering back at me are almost all men. True, in the last ten years I've been comforted by the faces of Elizabeth, Nicole, Jane, Meryl, Sophia, and some others. While the men may have been brilliant actors, they were not the human beings the women were, either in reliability, intelligence, or courage. Contrary to popular thought, women working together on films do not "cattily" compete with each other. On the contrary, they bond together, usually against an insensitive male in power. On *Steel Magnolias,* our director Herb Ross was consistently unkind to Dolly Parton and to newcomer Julia Roberts. The rest of us called him on it. The movie was fantastic and Julia went on to become the biggest star in the world. Women communicate on the level of feelings and the heart. Men tend to stay on the surface level of logic and the brain. There was a well-known adage that went around the sets of Hollywood in the old days: Never marry an actress—she is so much more than a woman. Never marry an actor—he is so much less than a man.

But I must confess, I've always been attracted to my male co-stars. I found male actors very intriguing, particularly when it came to vanity. The vanity of male actors is an impossible wall to scale. They know it, too. Robert Mitchum was a lesson in contradiction for me. He often seemed to be embarrassed by the makeup man or the camera director placing his chiseled face in a more favorable light. He would make self-deprecating jokes about his face, but when he walked away it would most assuredly be done in the Mitchum stride and strut—the "don't mess with me, I'm a tough guy who rode the rails with the hobos" body language. His voice, which he boomed as a throwaway over his shoulder, had a well-practiced lower register. Yes, he was a man's man in his own mind, but I saw something different. He used to say, "I'll do this piece-of-shit script just so someone else won't have to.

Better me than them." He was an extremely intelligent man with total recall who didn't need to spend much time memorizing lines or on character analysis. But his lumbering body language seemed to cover what he didn't want exposed. He didn't like to fight. Didn't like to argue (he chose to pontificate instead), and where his ability to make important choices was concerned, I'd have to say he was an emotional coward. All of his physical body art, his voice, his point of view, while demonstrating his version of himself, actually served to cover his deepest secret—he couldn't decide anything. He was essentially passive. Life *happened* to him. I *happened* to him. He rarely *made* anything happen.

He had been a pinup favorite of mine when I was a teenager. I loved his huge body and his way of moving on screen; it looked as though he were striding under water. His angular face and protective arms made me swoon. So when he was cast as Jerry opposite me in *Two for the Seesaw,* I was granted the pleasure of getting to know my teenage dream, assessing him from a grown-up point of view. I fell for him deeply. One of the wonderful things about making movies is that you get to either burst the bubble of your own fantasies or keep them intact. With him I had a little of each, until I realized he was fascinating but not the right man for me. It's probably a sign of maturity to go ahead and burst those bubbles—but it's more fun to keep your fantasies intact if you can!

A movie set is the most openhearted of environments in which to get to know someone and also, sometimes, to fall in love. First of all, the expression of human emotion is what a movie is about. So to that end each person cast understands that he or she needs to get to the bottom not only of the character but of him- or herself. Second, there is a lot of time in between setups to explore the feelings, conflicts, and insecurities of whomever you're working with. Third, everyone on the set knows that whatever happens there stays there. The crew knows it, the actors know it, and so does the front office. Once you leave the set and do whatever you do in the real world, there is no such protection.

So you have an environment where emotions are discussed and experimented with openly; there is a lot of time to indulge in exploring who you are, who you aren't, and who you want to become; and you are protected from gossip because these are the rules of the game. And a game it is—like life— a game about the game of life. That's why everyone on the outside wants to know about what happens on a set.

When filming a love scene, if an aggressive actor takes off all of his clothes and jumps on top of the leading lady, who may or may not peel off hers in turn—the crew will go right on lighting and moving equipment, the director will wave his hand to keep filming and say, "Okay, this is good for the characters," the publicist will roll his eyes and wonder how to deal with TMZ, the front office will immediately hear about it and start to gossip—and if the two underclad actors actually do like each other—who knows? Life is a movie anyway. (By the way, the above story really happened . . . and it's happened among many co-stars . . . sometimes including me . . . but that's another story.)

What happens when some of the most beautiful people on earth are physically and emotionally close is the topic that fills most of the tabloids every single week. It's a rare and mature relationship that survives *after* the romance of the fantasy world of movie makeup is gone. I know. It happened to me quite often. Most husbands and wives of actors and actresses know it's just a waiting game—if they can keep their jealousies under control and make patience the rule of the day.

I think I loved studying the actors I was involved with because I had such a complicated father. I was attracted to men who were equally complicated. Trying to understand them gave me plenty to do. I was a one-woman search party looking for a glimpse of who the man I loved at the time really was. They certainly didn't know any more about themselves than I did. They avoided their own search by becoming other men on the screen. I, in turn, avoided mine by searching for them in lieu of myself. Therefore, I never really took acting all that seriously. I acted when the director yelled "Action." In those early days of my career, I never thought much about the script or the part I was playing. I just did it when I did it. But the search for who someone else *really* was became a never-ending pleasure and pursuit for me. In a way, acting was a means for me to explore other people.

Later, when I worked with Yves Montand, I became fascinated with the intellectual art of singing and acting. He had

just come off a love affair with Marilyn Monroe. That fascinated me too, because I had heard so much about what went
on with her when making Billy Wilder's films. I was also a
great admirer of Simone Signoret. To be close to Yves meant
learning more about Simone. We did *My Geisha* together. We
shot it entirely in Japan, which was a culture none of us was
familiar with. So we were each splashed up against a foreign
environment, forcing us to cling together on the all-Japanese
set in order to understand what was going on.

As I look back on all my romantic movie-world relationships, which seem to always be so intriguing to the civilian
world, sex was basically a non-issue. To me and the man
involved, it was more about exploring identity and communi-
cating emotionally. On that basis, so much can be learned that
is valuable and growth-producing. The bugaboo of sex can
interfere with real communication because it is so complicated
and fraught with guilt and power plays and acting, no matter
how physically satisfying it can be.

As a person whose hobby *and* vocation has been the study
of character and human nature for seventy-six years, I feel
qualified to expostulate on the subject of leading men—and I
don't just mean actors. I ultimately had more relationships with
journalists and political leaders than with fellow actors. I think
I was slumming in power. I wanted to know what it felt like to
be able to help entire societies (as political leaders can do) or to
blow the whistle on those same politicians to keep them honest
(as journalists can do). I will never get over any of them.

I'm Not Over My Wall
of Life. I'm Under It.

I sit gazing up at the photographs that speak of the cast of characters in my life and times. They are so varied—from pictures of my childhood to pictures taken just a few months ago.

There are my parents, my parents' parents, my early dancing school teachers, my teenage years of cheerleading, me with the high school football captain, and school performances. My early years in New York as a dance student and then as a chorus dancer in *Oklahoma* (subway circuit at age 16!) and *Me and Juliet*. Sometimes I look at these pictures, peer into the past, and feel that it's all happening now. I even have the picture of myself and other chorus dancers from *Pajama Game* as we walked the rocky shores of Jones Beach. It was taken the afternoon before the night I had to go on for Carol Haney without a rehearsal of any kind.

I was half an hour late at the theater, and stretched across the stage door entrance were Jerry Robbins, Bob Fosse, Hal

Prince, and George Abbott (that's a picture I don't have but can see in my mind as clear as anything). They were frantic because Haney had twisted her ankle and couldn't walk, much less perform. I didn't know the lines, the song lyrics, or the dances. All I could think was: "I'm going to drop the hat in '*Steam Heat.*'"

Thoughts became reality. I dropped the hat and said "Shit," right out loud. The front row gasped.

With the help of all the cast members I got through the show and received a standing ovation at the curtain call. Strangely, I never felt so lonely. I was on my own with no idea what I was doing. Somehow, though, I felt I had my own angel on my shoulder who would be there for the rest of my life.

There are the greats from Hollywood splashed across my walls with stories and events written all over their faces as they gaze down at me.

Alfred Hitchcock, bless his soul (which is something I think he was lacking, by the way) was the master of cynical comedy. His first words to me on the set were, "Genuine chopper, old girl, genuine chopper." *The Trouble with Harry* was my first film and I didn't know what he meant. When I said, "Excuse me, Mr. Hitchcock?" he just looked at me and said it again. John Forsythe (my co-star) came to my aid. "It's Cockney slang," he explained. "Try and put together the meaning of the individual words."

I thought of a synonym for "genuine" and came up with

"real." I didn't know what to do with chopper. John made a sign like a hatchet movement. The hatchet move suggested "axe." Put together, the words said "real-axe." Relax. Oh my God, I thought. Is this how he directs actors?

The shoot commenced. Hitch was famous for thinking actors were irrelevant. "The only important things," he said, "are the script and the first preview." Right.

He lived up to that way of thinking, though he did give me one other piece of direction. "Before you say that line," he told me one day, "dog's feet."

Oh dear, what were dog's feet?

Of course. Dog's feet were paws. "Before you say that line, pause." That was it.

My relationship with Hitch was not about acting. It was about food. I remember he told me about a kitchen he had designed. He had paced out the smallest kitchen needed to make a good meal, then he had the kitchen designed to fit the same number of steps he had walked . . . the fewer the better. He knew how many steps from the fridge to the stove to the table.

He had such a dark sense of humor that I'm not sure even now that he's really dead. What would an actor know anyway? To him we were cattle. The first day of a picture with him, the actress Carole Lombard greeted him from the center of a corral she'd had the crew knock together for her. He thought it was funny. And true.

Hitch taught me how to eat well, and to think of something

funny when I was scared. Maybe that's the best piece of direction I've ever gotten, given the state of the world today.

Dean and Jerry were a lesson in how *not* to break up. I did their second-to-last picture with them. By that time, they couldn't stand each other. Dean was really the spontaneous funny one, and Jerry was more of a scientist of comedy who wanted to be a director. I was caught in the middle, as were the rest of the cast and crew. Many times the producer Hal Wallis (who was worse than anyone) had to come to the set and insist that time was money and the two of them should get on with it.

Dean's soft-spoken personality made it hard to tell when he was really upset. I never saw him angry or anything like that. He was just trying to get through each day. Jerry basically took over, and when the next picture in their contract came around, Dean simply walked. I had the same agent as both of them, so I heard the details of the breakup. There was a script meeting with the two of them and the writer to sketch out a comedy scene involving some sort of police chase. Jerry controlled the meeting and said he wanted to flip it and have them chase the police. Apparently Dean said, "Oh no, that would never happen. In my experience, the only time I've ever seen the police is in my rearview mirror." Jerry said, "Your character wouldn't act that way," and Dean said, "Well, then get somebody who will," and walked out. They didn't speak for twenty years until a charity event occurred and the same agent put them together again. Seeing them together again that evening was wonderful.

I worked with Dean alone after that in *All in a Night's Work*. I developed a crush on him but—thank goodness—his wife was always around. I was over the crush by the time we did *Some Came Running* together. By then I was more interested in who the mobsters were who always seemed to be on the lam around us. Sam Giancana taught me how to play gin rummy. He won by reading my cards in my glasses. I pulled a toy gun on him once because he took my cannoli. He went for his .45, pointed it at me, and Dean and Frank walked into the room. They fell down laughing. I didn't. That's when I realized who he was.

Dean and Frank were made for each other, and many, many women. I was not one of them, but I miss them both more than I want to think about. Hollywood will never see the likes of them again. They were the real deal. By the way, it was Dean who really knew the mob guys and told them to go away. Frank was what they called a "wannabe." I was a mascot they protected. I was never quite sure from whom!

In 1957, Mike Todd gave a party at Madison Square Garden for 18,000 of his closest friends. He wanted me to go to New

York and ride an elephant while throwing hot dogs out to the crowd. The studio wouldn't let me go (insurance reasons), so he and Elizabeth Taylor had to make do without me. I used to watch him operate on the telephone as he was putting projects together. He excelled in the longtime technique of telling one person he had another already lined up and vice versa. Everyone believed him, because he had pulled it off before. I think he was a reincarnation of P. T. Barnum.

My times with the two Jacks (Lemmon and Nicholson) were filled with fun, teasing, spontaneity, and really good acting, but we never socialized much off the set. They were the professional acting loves of my life. Lemmon was always intricately prepared. Nicholson never knew what he would do. I enjoyed both approaches. It was the cinematic art of opposites. Lemmon loved to be acknowledged and liked having his picture taken. Nicholson would twist his body and move in another direction if he suspected a camera was anywhere nearby.

I now have a third Jack in my life. I've just finished a picture with Jack Black called *Bernie*. It was a pleasure to go to work with him every day. In poker or in life, three Jacks is hard to beat.

Danny Kaye smiles down at me. When I was shooting a film with Vittorio De Sica in Paris, Danny came to visit me.

Once he got there, he decided he wanted to fly me to New York for dinner at a Chinese restaurant he knew very well. In fact, he often cooked meals there himself. That's what he did that night. He piloted the plane across the Atlantic himself, cooked dinner for me, and flew me back to Paris to be ready for work the next day. Why was I so foolhardy where my professional life was concerned? I don't know. I did such things often in the middle of a shoot. I guess getting every experience I could out of life was absolutely as important to me as having a successful career.

Danny would often fly me to dinner at a good steak house regardless of where I was shooting or where the restaurant was. He also completely remodeled my kitchen, much to the chagrin of the couple who worked for me. I still cook some of the meals he taught me and think sweet thoughts of him.

We had a fabulous relationship, full of love, starlit night skies, food, and humor. Just before he died he insisted he didn't want a funeral, so it never happened.

My Walls of Life still sing and they sing of talent and longevity. I often think of what I'd do to protect the pictures if I had to make a quick getaway. Would Streisand (we're born on the same day), Kidman, Siegfried & Roy, Glenn Ford, Debbie Reynolds, Sharon Stone, George C. Scott, Jane Fonda, Michael Caine, Robert Downey Jr., Paul Newman, Anthony Hopkins, Nick Cage, and Elizabeth Taylor come with me?

As I grow older, I find myself reevaluating experiences on my walls and relating to them in the spirit of synchronicity. I'm understanding that nothing is truly random. Somehow, in each of our lives is evidence of the scenario and destiny we have outlined for ourselves in order to discover who we really are, why we did what we did, and where our souls have actually been. These memories (and so many others, including those of past lives) are part of my consciousness now. Is all time occurring at once, as Einstein said? When we have a particularly vivid memory, aren't people from our past with us in the present? Everything is part of the now, we can touch past and future simultaneously and get a glimpse of this important truth.

Perhaps it is by design that with age our short-term memory disappears and long-term memory is more present, because it is necessary to resolve and come to terms with our lives so we can understand why we created them in the first place. I drive down a freeway and suddenly I'm on the street before it became a freeway. Where I was going and what happened when I got there rushes back to me with urgent importance. *Remember . . . remember . . .*

The people from my life are suddenly important to me in different ways and for different reasons than I realized when I was with them. Did I really choose to know them before I was born? Did I actually already know the souls of the people in these pictures and together we are devising a learning process to help one another understand ourselves and each other more completely? Are strangers just old friends we don't quite remember?

One intelligent friend told me years ago that I shouldn't delve with too much curiosity into the "unanswerable" mysteries of life or it could lead to insanity. I really listened to what this friend was saying to me, but I just can't feel that having a strong sense of curiosity is a bad thing. I have always felt safe *because* I was curious.

I feel that I am encapsulating the magical, mythical, mystery tour of my life now because I am preparing to let go of the past with a deeper understanding of what it meant and why I wrote the scenarios in the first place. I will soon be ready for a new consciousness. I am tired of the word "consciousness," but I can't find a better one to substitute for it yet. "Beingness" doesn't really work either. I know there is a new beginning coming because we can't go on the way we are. It is dispiriting and soul searing to the extreme. I have come to understand that spirit and soul are the only permanent truths that matter.

I Am Over Fear Taught
in the Name of Religion

I never cease to be amazed at how far some religious people will go in order to turn their destinies over to God rather than take charge of them themselves. If the Devil really does exist, he would beat his chest with pride at how significant we humans have made him. More movies and books have been made heralding his existence than anyone else . . . because the fear of him makes so much money. Fear seems to be the most communal human emotion, and the easiest to exploit. Fear of God, fear of the Devil, fear of terrorists, fear of death, fear of life, fear of race, fear, fear, fear. Learn how to propagandize fear and you can control a civilization and make a lot of money.

I believe I always traveled alone because I wanted to force myself to get over the fear that had been inculcated in me of daring too much. So my relationship with fear has never been paralyzing. I lived to travel to places where there was conflict because I wanted to learn how to problem solve. I can't say I learned how to solve much, but I have learned a great deal about how conflicts come about.

In the early sixties I went to Mississippi to understand what Stokely Carmichael and Rap Brown meant when they said the United States of America was born with people who had a gun in one hand and a Bible in the other. I met Rap and listened to the complaints and the well-intentioned protests of the Black Panthers. I understood their anger and their propensity for violence. Then I met John Lewis. He was then, and remains to this day, a saintly human being. He accepted my need to understand, and I think the fact that I was a lone white woman in the middle of the Civil Rights movement in Mississippi made him want to understand me on another level. He arranged for me to live with a black family in Issaqueena County, Mississippi, so I could see for myself what it meant to live as a black person in the South of that time. I stayed with Unida Blackwell and her family for close to a week. I listened to them describe their lives. I cooked with them and prayed with them. Nearly everything they ate was drizzled with Karo Syrup. That's how they grew up. Their bathroom was an outhouse. That's how they grew up. They had to heat their water on the stove if they wanted a bath. That's how they grew up. They were generous and sharing and funny. That's how they grew up.

One night toward the end of my time there, I looked out a window and saw the Ku Klux Klan burning a cross in front of their small shack. The cross was the Klan's instrument of fear and destruction. Unida and I and her family stayed inside and sang gospel hymns, waiting for morning light when I could leave. That burning cross was a sign that my presence was no longer going to be tolerated, and I couldn't bear for Unida's family to be in greater danger because of me.

In fact, everywhere I have traveled in the world, the conflicts I've seen stemmed from organized religion in one way or another.

My travels in North Africa and the Middle East were most revealing. I spent a great deal of time in Tunisia and I even bought a piece of beachfront property there in Hammamet. Under Bourguiba, Tunisia was a Muslim democracy. As a result, its entrance into the modern industrialized world was gentler than that of some of its neighbors. The people I met and became friendly with often traveled to Europe. Some were Christian. I remember taking Tarak Ben Amar, then a young boy, to school in Rome. He has since become quite a powerful figure in the North African and European film industry, financing, developing, and overseeing many films and television series.

There was never talk of religion when I was together with my Arabic friends. We talked of new ideas, business deals, creative projects, and the like. God was a private matter and history was a favorite topic of conversation, not dogma. That held true in my travels to Morocco and throughout the Middle East. In Egypt I slept in the giant sarcophagus of the Great Pyramid and learned about the Egyptian empire. In

Turkey, I learned of the Catholic ecumenical meetings held in Constantinople in AD 553 where the teachings of physical reembodiment (reincarnation) were struck from the New Testament on orders from Empress Theodora of Byzantium. She single-handedly erased our spiritual history. I had a past-life experience as a harem girl in the home of a pasha in Turkey and became physically nauseous with the memory of my confinement and lack of freedom. I learned how the major religions intersect and witnessed Coptic Christians living peacefully side by side with Muslims.

At Isfahan I had another past-life experience where I had entertained a large audience at the theater outside under the stars. I remembered how good the acoustics were and felt the warmth of the summer night. I can never pinpoint the actual dates of my past-life memories, only the environment . . . that is, except for the memories I recalled when I walked across Spain doing the Santiago de Compostela pilgrimage. That was an experience that altered my life because of the solitude of the walk. I walked ten hours a day for one month, slept in *refugios* (shelters), and begged for food. It helped me put my place in the world into proper perspective. My grandest lesson from that journey has been that of *allow* and *surrender*. Yes, I am an over-achiever with a sometimes bulldog-like work ethic, but when I walked across Spain by myself, begging for food and sleeping in shelters, I soon learned the art of surrender and allowance.

My pilgrimage along the Camino de Santiago de Compostela was one of the most influential undertakings I ever dared. I went alone, a woman in her sixth decade, walked alone for the most part (this was the most difficult), slept alone wherever I could find a *refugio* or shelter, and had my own thoughts for company. The Spanish paparazzi got word of what I was doing and I was ambushed a few times, which was quite unpleasant for me because I behaved like an insensitive bitch (I made one woman reporter cry) and threw a rock at a camera crew. The villagers began to understand I was not making the pilgrimage for publicity but only for spiritual reasons. After that, they began to point the paparazzi in the wrong direction.

I learned some essential lessons on my pilgrimage. All I really needed for physical comfort was a good pair of shoes, a hat to shield me from the sun, a little something to eat, and clean water. (Oh, one more thing. I hadn't realized how potassium depleted I would get, so I experienced severe cramping in my arms, legs, and hands. It was awful. For anyone who does this pilgrimage, take potassium tablets with you.) When it was time to rest, I needed a good sleeping bag and an attitude of whatever will be will be.

Nothing was as important as zeroing in on my innate ability to be content with myself, the land, the pain, my intentions, and the power of allowing. I felt in touch with the rhythm of nature for the first time. I could almost hear the trees breathe and the ground groan. I understood that phrase "being one with the all." The ground under me spoke of the ages, and I touched some past life incarnations that were funny fodder for Jay Leno. I call it cosmic humor when people make good-natured fun of me. I've finally come to realize everything is God's joke anyway. I'm just one of the characters in the comedy.

The other essential lesson I learned was that I walked too fast and didn't spend enough time processing each hour. I was wedded to the idea of completing the pilgrimage on July 4, American Independence Day. I started on June 4 and told myself I should be finished in exactly a month. That was a goal with no "let it be" intelligence to it. Sometimes goal orientation can destroy a deeper and more meaningful experience. Yes, my family and friends were worried if I was safe, and even sane, and I'd promised them it wouldn't take more than a month, but I should have done it all for me, however long it took. Besides, I found that I loved the unpredictability of being a guerrilla traveler.

Maybe that's what we do with our soul's journey from lifetime to lifetime. Maybe we choose our destiny but we never know exactly what we're getting into until we're actually there. So my journey in this lifetime with all its success, failure, fame, searching for my true identity, and exploring new lands, is a mirror of my soul's journey through time to understand not only who I am but who I was, and most of all, what is my relationship with the Creator. Where do I start and where does God stop, if there is such a place? Where does God begin and where do I continue? When I observe nature, animals, and even birds and bees seem to have no problem knowing where they fit and what their purpose is. Their intentions always seem admirable and in balance. Not so with humans.

The Camino was lonely when I was walking it in the present, but it was also peopled with memories of many incarnational experiences from the past. I remembered being a Muslim Gypsy girl who had migrated from Morocco and was living with the Coptic Christians in the hills of Spain. I remembered a cross I wore, which, when I presented it, protected me from the Muslims and the Christians alike. At one point in my present day walk, I was guided to a jewelry store in a small village along the Camino. I looked in the window and saw the cross I remembered from several hundred years before. I went in and questioned the proprietor. He gave me the same information I remembered from the past-life memory; it had belonged to a Gypsy girl (me) from Morocco and she had used it for protection. I bought the cross (my only purchase on the trek) and always take it with me when I leave home.

What I was learning about religion around the world as I traveled was that it afforded each denomination and culture an opportunity to bypass responsibility for itself and assign that task to God. Since each culture has its own history of violence with an "enemy," it is easy to make that enemy an adversary to their God. Since we all anthropomorphize God in our human image, let's make God's adversary a pitch-forked human-looking fellow, too: even better—someone who bears a resemblance to our rival tribe or long-held enemy. This evil

Devil we'd made was not only what made us humans unhappy, it was what made "our" God unhappy. We invented this outside evil and could justify any behavior toward him by saying we were trying to protect our God. We humans weren't capable of becoming God-like enough to neutralize the entire conflict.

Therefore, I gave up religion a long time ago. I'm over all that religion thing and have been ever since I put my experiences with my own karma (past-life recollections) together with my strong sense of self-responsibility.

As I conversed with people everywhere, I found that most of them had had a déjà vu experience. Rather than relating to such things as life-learning experiences of reality, they generally put them aside in the category of paranormal: beyond comprehension and, in some cases, crazy-making. It was as though they thought God wouldn't like it . . .

Empress Theodora had exercised her authority well. She wanted to be the judge in the Justinian time period of what was real and what wasn't. The great Greek philosopher Origen had been teaching the meaning of reincarnational karma all his life: "What one sows, so does one reap." "All energy returns to its source." Scientific spirituality . . . more the truth than anything else I've come across. So we humans, both individually and collectively, continue to follow the dictates of our religion and/or culture, making the same violent missteps in violence and war, when in reality no one ever dies, they just change form. The soul goes on to another level of understanding until it is ready to return to its physical reembodiment journey again. Therefore, war itself is crazy. No one ever dies, they just incur more karma.

It has always made so much logical sense to me. And such a journey of the soul does *not* rule out God: the God of light, the God of love, and the God of balance and justice. The laws of karma make cosmic justice a reality. One may not reap what one sows in the same lifetime, but he or she will reap what has been sown eventually—even Hitler. (Hitler is everybody's favorite monster to question or elucidate the reality of soul.) I remember visiting with Mother Teresa in India at her home for the dying. She said her reason for devoting her life to helping others was when she realized she had a part of Hitler in her. Those were her words. She became a saint because she exercised her self-responsibility, not because she was somehow completely good and pure. (No one is.)

Once on a plane from India, I was seated next to Jawaharlal Nehru, the great Indian statesman. A fly had worked its way into the cabin. I went to swat it, and he stopped me. "You never know. That fly could have been your grandmother!"

Yes, there was much for me to learn in India. The Hindu religion had a lot to teach me in terms of the spiritual sciences: yoga, meditation, diet, reincarnation, and the power of passive resistance. When I left India to visit the Himalayan kingdom of Bhutan, I knew I was in for many lessons.

First of all, I contracted a parasite (some people have told me it must have been cholera) and was sick for two weeks while living in an open lean-to in the middle of winter.

I thought I was going to die and reverted to the only thing I understood to prevent myself from freezing to death: mind over matter. I meditated on an inner sun within my solar plexus. I concentrated very hard the way I do when I become a character I'm playing. Just as I believe I'm the character, I believed I possessed a very healing inner sun, an inner intense light. Soon I realized I was perspiring and felt perfectly warm. To this day, whenever I feel very cold, I still do that. It takes practice, but more to the point, it takes a self-responsible attitude and firm belief that I create and control my own reality. Sometimes that reality becomes the reality of what I've lived at some other time and place.

I have developed an understanding that I am part of the web of God and light, and if I just let go and let God, I will tread the path of my own designated destiny. I am responsible for my life and destiny because I signed up for it before I came in. I chose my parents and all my relatives in order to learn some cosmic and spiritual life lessons this time around. With this understanding, I don't blame any of them for what happened in my childhood or what happens to me as an adult. I find myself always aided by a synchronicity of events and people. If I need to know something and don't know where to go, I find someone popping up in my life who informs me of that very thing. If I want to find someone but don't know how to reach them, they often call me out of the blue. If I feel physically sick, I ask my higher self what caused it. And I always get some kind of answer. I'll take that over a fear-based religion any day.

I'm Over People Who Repeat Themselves (When I Didn't Want to Hear What They Said in the First Place)

This repeating what you just said business is developing into a national sickness. I guess people feel they are not being heard. Or maybe they repeat what they say in order to decide whether they really mean it.

Just as I am ready to respond to what someone has said, he or she repeats it. And whenever I ask a question, for example: "Can you tell me where I can get a good meal that is organic?" they say, "You want a good meal that is organic?" . . . beat, beat . . . "You want to know a place where you can get a good meal that is organic?"

I usually answer with something like, "Where did you hear that?"

I go berserk and I can't help myself. Is this what they call echolalia? People only seem to want to hear the echo of what they think and say.

I'll Never Get Over Trying to Understand the Russian Soul

The Soviet Union in 1962 was an example of extreme imbalance, which was necessary to get over as soon as possible. The imbalance in Russia was so extreme it could actually seem comic. I was in Romania for the premiere of *The Apartment,* and on a whim I decided to go, via Intourist, to the Soviet Union. Intourist, the official state travel agency of the USSR, was a joke. It was entirely staffed by the KGB. The people who were assigned to "manage" me and my girlfriend Lori's trip spied on us, tried to blackmail us, and finally, because we missed a train from Leningrad to Moscow, stole my luggage, leaving me without a passport, clothes, or any travel papers.

Lori and I got ourselves smuggled into Leningrad University, where the students were having anti-Catholic week. What was funny was they mixed up Catholic values with Nazi German values. I laughed out loud even though I never have been a fan of the Pope and what he stands for. There were posters throughout the university equating Hitler with the Pope. There were official discussions and seminars on said subject, and while I was there, there were also two days and nights of off-the-record conversation in the barracks with black bread and a few bottles of scotch someone else had smuggled in to sustain us.

The students weren't really all that curious about Nazi religious propaganda, or about the outside world in general. That's what surprised me more than anything. Where was their curiosity? Had it been squelched along with their individual freedoms? They were interested in what I could tell them about the latest rock-and-roll music, which at least said something about their preferred art form.

The stifling suffocation of curiosity and inquiry overwhelmed me after a while. It produced an even more profound urge toward rebellion in me, and when we finally snuck out of the university to return to our hotel, I was told we no longer had a room and that my luggage had been removed by the authorities. Rather than sleep on a threadbare sofa in the freezing cold lobby of the rundown hotel, I made myself purposely uncomfortable on the icy floor. Benny Goodman and his orchestra were in town, so of course he was being followed by a Western reporter. The two of them entered the lobby, recognized me attempting to sleep on the floor, and wanted to know what was going on. I told them the entire story, including a coda which made headlines in the Russian papers later: "I want to come back to the Soviet Union in the winter and dance the can-can nude in Red Square."

Two years before, Nikita Khrushchev, the Soviet premier, had visited the set of *Can-Can* on a tour of the Fox lot. He watched us dance it and then quipped to the U.S. papers, "The face of humanity is prettier than its backside." I countered by saying, "He was upset because we wore panties." (The can-can was performed in France without underwear; that was why it was considered risqué.) Later on, after seeing *The Apartment,* Khrushchev sent me a note. It simply said, "You've improved."

As you might imagine, my Soviet adventure was one I longed to get over, but I found I couldn't. It felt as though so much of Russia itself was buried inside a deeper memory somewhere inside me.

Years later, I had a complicated, loving relationship with a Soviet director I will call Vassy. He was from an elite Russian family and longed to come to the West to work. I was his unofficial sponsor and found him to be exhilarating, adorable, impossibly difficult, deeply religious, unbelievably chauvinistic, and a profound believer in evil. We fought and argued about everything (I believe now just for the sake of the challenge). We hiked, laughed, and saw movies, and I learned to cook Russian food—kasha, beets, garlic, cabbage—and of course, to drink vodka. Vassy was a very well-educated artist who managed to get hold of caviar and God knows what else, and yet he dried his socks on a teakettle.

He was certain he had lived many times before (with me, actually). Most of his leading actresses and one of his wives looked like me. He attended many channeling sessions with me. It was through Vassy that I came to know of the Soviet government's acceptance of the presence of UFOs and of extraterrestrial life visiting Earth, and he was instrumental in my visiting Billy Meier in Switzerland, whose abduction story is the most provable UFO case on record. Through Vassy, I met Roald Sagdaev, the head of the Soviet Space Agency at the time, and was told that UFOs were documented fact, alien spacecraft had visited earth, and that a cover-up was in place so as not to alarm the human race.

Vassy and I were compatible in so many ways, with the exception of the obsessive belief he had in the existence of evil. He could not wrap his mind around the possibility that humans determined their own negative reality all on their own. He called it "evil interference." When we argued vociferously, he would often take my shoulders, shake me, and say "Shirlitchka, you are being possessed by the Devil." He couldn't accept that the "Devil" was my own negative thinking running amok in my own mind.

He believed we humans were put on Earth to fight and win the battle against EVIL (when he said it, it always sounded like all capital letters to me), the Devil, Satan, call it what you will. When I tried to reason with him by explaining that the Aramaic translation of the words Satan and Evil was simply "that which is not well for you," it made no impact. The etymology of words is important, but he was unshakably convinced (through his religion) that the Devil existed as an outside force. For a sophisticated man from such an intellectual, worldly family, I felt he should have gotten over a belief in the Devil a long time ago. He couldn't do it. When we parted ways, he gave me his family Bible and said it should remain with me. It has, and it always will.

When considering our American relationship with Russia today, I find my experience of having lived with a Soviet invaluable. Vassy considered himself part Muslim. His first wife was Muslim and he was extremely drawn to Islamic history and considered part of the Russian soul to be Islamic. I understood what he meant because so much of the Soviet Union was Muslim. He talked of how his country was an amalgamation of two religious cultures.

Since the Berlin Wall came down, I'm not sure much has really changed on the inside of the Russian people, in their soul. Despite the decades of living under the Soviet regime, many Russians remain as much in thrall to religious orthodoxy as their ancestors. I feel that any deep belief in orthodox religion can be a bridge to understanding each other, but it is also very likely a bridge down a path of destruction. Vassy's core belief that Evil and the Devil exist as literal entities that can be fought and defeated was impossible for me to countenance. He knew most of the Soviet leaders and said they all secretly wore crosses around their necks, even though they claimed that religion was the opiate of the people. That told me that they, like Vassy, also believed deeply in the Devil. Violent, hateful acts could always be excused as the work of the Devil. It was as if taking responsibility for our own behavior was not an option since that could all be left up to God. For me, the most troubling aspect of Vassy's belief system was that he felt we humans should devote our lives to protecting God (Allah) from this so-called Devil. Only destruction and violence can follow such a belief, I believe.

The Soviet Union may be no more, but Russia is eternal. Without understanding as best we can how the deep roots of two ancient religions inform many Russians' thoughts and actions, as well as their art and culture, we are only witnessing a shadow play while the real actors and their underlying motivations remain undiscovered.

I Am (Almost) Over
Watching the News

As I watch the news each night, I try to gain a greater understanding of what's happening to us humans on our beloved planet. But more and more these days the news is mostly homogenized and without any objectivity or perspective. If we've seen one news program, we've seen them all . . . even Fox News. It's the same news stories, just told in another (and often more colorful and entertaining) way. That's why they have high ratings. But Bill O'Reilly is a bully for profit. He's ridiculous. I've done his show because I asked to be on it. I remember a dinner I had with him and some other power brokers in New York. At one point he turned to me and said, "My God, you are actually a nice person. You aren't stuck-up and acting like a celebrity." I wish I had a snapshot of my face at that moment. Was he kidding or what? He was so small-town prejudiced.

When I went on his show he walked into the greenroom, imposing his significant height over my face, and said he was surprised I showed up. I said, "Bill, I asked to be on your show to promote my book, *Sage-ing While Age-ing,* because I know you are interested in UFOs and what the real story might be."

He puffed himself up even further and without missing a beat he said, "We are going to talk about the war in Iraq and how you Hollywood people think you know it all."

I was fascinated to see how he steeled himself to get ready to go into attack mode. I protested that I didn't want to talk about Iraq and he knew that from the preshow interview. He ordered me to sit down (his chair was a foot higher than mine) at his table and proceeded to berate me because I was from Hollywood. I told him I was from Virginia and could meet his patriotism any day. I said it wasn't patriotic of us Americans to invade a country just because we didn't like their despotic, cruel dictator. He went on to defend the war and to attack some of my friends in Hollywood on their anti-war stance, saying that they didn't know enough about it to have an opinion—"and you don't either," he finally finished.

"No shit, Bill," I said. "I'm not a military commander. So I'm not going to talk about it. I want to talk about UFOs and some of your opinions on such things." He said, "You admit you don't know about how to conduct a war in Iraq?"

"Yes, Bill. No shit. I already told you that."

When I said "shit" he didn't know how to react. I think he was worried that his show would be bleeped. Later, I told him that the most disgusting aspect of his TV interviews was how most of his guests sucked up to him in return for his having them appear on his show. They would laugh nervously and never get mad or upset with him—another example of how dumbed-down and intimidated we've become in the face of right-wing power.

I've often thought about how he prepared himself for verbal battle like an actor who prepares for a scene. I remembered the bullying side he showed the world when his sex scandal and all that soaping up in the shower were made public. It made me suspect he is a more complicated and interesting man than his abusive, bullying politics would suggest. He'd be good for a reality porno show.

I like to get my news by holding a newspaper, but lately I've become reluctant to contribute to the cutting down of more trees so I subscribe to *The Wall Street Journal, The New York Times, Los Angeles Times, New York Daily News, New York Post, Time,* and *Newsweek* on the web. On television I watch CNN, BBC, Fox, NBC, CBS, ABC, and MSNBC for news. I don't like the clubby, bubbly, locker room atmosphere that the morning news shows have gotten into just to make us feel better and to suggest they are hosted by friendly, cheerful, real people. All it makes me think is: these news sets are where they actually live; these are the only people they know . . . day after day, hour after hour. I think of them going into makeup and hair and deciding if it would be counterproductive to change their image. Do they have stylists and press agents to orchestrate how they are perceived when they feed us "real" news?

The whole world is show business now, and Obama is the prime example. What a family man, what a nice guy, what a patient intellect he has while his advisors do the necessary dirty work. His speeches are magnificently acted, but what would he be without a teleprompter? He has good writers, good comedy punchers, and an extraordinary capacity to maintain quiet dignity while he must be scared to death over what is happening in the world. Who is he really? Does he want to be president of the planet as some say his speeches in the Mideast, Germany, France, and England seem to indicate? Was he "chosen" by the global banking elite in the world because he can be made to see so many differing points of view? Is it beneficial that his family background is partly Muslim, which could be good for fostering world peace? Why is that such a scary idea to some people? Would he, in the last analysis, be in favor of a one-world currency and a one-world government? Does he have the tools to be a great unifier, or is he fated only to divide the country further? More to the point, is one-world government a good idea?

These are all questions that will never be answered—or even considered—by our current mainstream news organizations, but they deserve to be.

I Am Over Politics. It's Jazz. And I'm Over All That Jazz.

The George McGovern experience with Watergate, the break-in itself, the abuses of power by our FBI and CIA—that was enough for me. I spent a year and a half campaigning for George. The Nixon people made it clear to me that I was an enemy; my apartment in New York was ransacked beyond recognition, and the telephone lines cut to ensure that I got the message. I wasn't on the "show business enemies" list; I was on the "political enemies" list. My phones were bugged by the Americans, the Swedes (I was having a relationship with their prime minister), the Russians (having a relationship with a Russian director), and the Aussies (having a relationship with the Australian foreign minister). My phone lines were not private and under constant surveillance until I became very serious (and chatty) about my metaphysics, the science of the soul, and the potential reality of our being visited by a more advanced interplanetary intelligence. That's when everybody left me alone and decided I was wacky. Except, I think, for military intelligence. I believe I am still being surveyed in every way by military intelligence, just in case one of those ships from a far-off planet picks me up one day.

Anyway, I am over everything that involves politics. What happens to me spiritually is far more important to me now.

When I watch the show business–like broadcasts of the news, I'm aware of a deliberate manipulation of the stories in service to higher ratings. At least Rupert Murdoch admits it. But the difference between any foreign news programs and ours is striking. We are not global thinkers. We are globally oriented only in the sense of caring about an international event in light of how it relates to us.

When I hear the controversy about sending more troops to Afghanistan, nobody but Christiane Amanpour mentions the value and power of the poppy fields and the opium trade. Who wouldn't want to control the country where as much as 90 percent of the world's heroin production is located? Why don't our newscasters get past the point of imposing democracy on another tribal culture and get to the real point of why we're there? Follow the money, as the old saying goes.

Let's have some deep and probing investigative reporting on *why* so many people are addicted to drugs. If we did that I think we'd be into an investigation of the contemporary human spirit, of depression, of pointlessness, of spiritual poverty, and finally the addiction to serving whatever God we've been taught to believe in, whether it's the Christian one, the

Islamic one, or any other. We know that more killing has occurred in the name of "God" than anything else. Did the Devil make us do it? Let's investigate who we really are in relation to our beliefs, because if we don't we are going to be forever manipulated by the real ruling elite in this world—the international banking community. In effect, "they" understand the real polarities governing our lives are not Good versus Evil, but rather Materialism versus Spirit.

I Am Over Young People Who Are Rude

In recent years, we've become so technology-obsessed that good manners probably belong in antiquity. When we leave a message for someone, we tell ourselves that we don't need to be nice because we're only talking to a machine anyway. But almost everyone I see out in the world today appears mad, put out, and in general they regard you as a pain in the butt if you're over 50. It's as though everyone comes from New York City.

The shop clerks wish you'd never come in, even though their shop is going broke.

The coffee vendors are simply cappuccino orderers with nothing to say to help pass the time.

The cash register clerks in the supermarket ring you up as though Al Qaeda is around the corner and they need to win "beat the clock" against the register and get out.

The people in Radio Shack don't know what electronics are.

Waiters in restaurants have the amazing ability to avoid eye contact the moment you think you'd like the check or some service.

Young people who are out of work and want jobs won't work for less pay than the maximum they think they can get. They feel entitled.

The young people are the leaders of the Rude Pack. I know the rest of us have screwed up the world, but I wouldn't want to leave it to them anyway.

I Will Never Get Over Africa

My time in Africa lives with me always. I will never forget the magic of such a place. More than any other place I've been, I wish to return to Africa. I would like to live on a wild game reserve and observe the animals all day. That would make me truly happy.

When I was there, I lived among the Masai of East Africa and what was then Tanganyika (now Tanzania). I initially went to Africa to visit Robert Mitchum, with whom I was having a relationship. He was shooting a movie there. It wasn't long before I became more interested in what I was seeing and learning than I was in Robert and the movie. I wandered off. Certain highlights stand out for me, things that I will never get over as long as I live.

The particular tribe of Masai I met had never seen a white person before. They could identify with my freckles, which they believed would someday grow together in order to make me more brown. They were friendly and wanted me to know them. They invited me to help birth a baby, where the mother waited for me inside a hut. There was a fire in the middle of the dirt floor, smoke wafting everywhere as flies darted and landed on the mother giving birth, the newborn, the placenta, and me. Other women surrounded the baby as the mother chewed the umbilical cord away. Then the women handed the baby around the circle as each attending woman followed the custom of spitting in its mouth to welcome it (a girl) to the *menyatta* (the village). When the child was handed to me, I couldn't do it. I didn't want to contaminate the baby with whatever I might have brought from the Western world. The women seemed to understand. The mother asked my name. I said "Shirley." She promptly named the child Shurri. I was honored.

Flash forward fifteen years later. I was doing a book signing in San Francisco. A young woman came up to me, handed me a ring, and said, "Hello again, my name is Shurri. You were there when I was born."

How should I relate to this? She handed me a picture to prove that I'd been there. Synchronicity as a fact, not a coincidence, was becoming more of a reality every day. A year later, a man appeared at my doorstep in Encino. He handed me three stones, which he said came from the chieftain of the Masai tribe I spent so much time with. The chief wanted to be remembered to me. The man who brought me the stones was the man whom I ultimately went to Peru to visit. He was the person who said he had had encounters with extraterrestrials in the Andes Mountains. I could see the reality of the web of synchronicity in my life. Out of the Peruvian visit came *Out on a Limb*, which I think helped birth a New Age spiritual movement.

I still have the ring from Shurri, and I had the stones from the Masai chieftain mounted in a triangular shape, which I not only treasure but also feel protects me.

I was besotted by Africa—the animals, the Masai (who believe they are on Earth only to protect our planet's cattle), the landscapes, the miracles of nature I saw every day.

A few days after the birth of Shurri, I hired a plane to take me to Tanganyika and join what I thought was to be a photographic safari. The pilot turned up drunk in Nairobi, where we took off. So, on some level I had to help him land the plane on an isolated field in Tanganyika. I stepped out of the plane, not knowing where I was or where I was supposed to go to join the safari. Three Masai *morani* (warriors) came from the bushes. One of them said in English, "You are white woman named Shurri?" I nodded and followed him without asking any questions. What was I thinking in those days? Did I trust more than was wise? Did my middle-class "don't dare" upbringing make me an adventurer, inspiring me to challenge any circumstance? I really don't know. I do know I couldn't do that now, whether it's because I've gotten more cautious as I've aged, or because the world is a more dangerous place. And why is it more dangerous? Because there are too many people and there is an imbalance?

Yes, there is an imbalance now. Everybody knows it, feels

it. What can we do about it? The Masai are instructive on this point.

The Masai led me to the safari, which turned out to be a hunting safari, not photographic. The Masai stayed with me day and night as though protecting me. The safari people were nice enough. When I told the white hunters the Masai knew my name when I landed, they said it couldn't have been the use of smoke signals, and no one could run that fast from where I had been in Kenya. No, they said, it was their experience that the Masai had achieved the skill of thought transference. They were balanced with nature and nature's forms of communication, and it carried over into their human communication. The white hunters noticed that the Masai were always around me, following and observing, taking spiders out of my tent at night, protecting me, and they were intrigued. I seemed to be a character in a sophisticated primitive play I hadn't even read.

The documentaries that have been filmed in Africa do not do the place justice. It is a paradise of balance. For example: I could bear witness to the survival of the fittest on the part of the animals because the white hunters told me they believed that the souls of the animals who were the victims of the predators left their bodies before they were ripped apart for food. They said there was a kind of collective spiritual understanding among all the animals relating to food and life. It was a spiritual game of survival because none of the animals really died anyway. Only their bodies did. As long as the game of predator and victim was played for life survival, it was part of the natural balance. I tweaked on the name the humans gave the animals: "game." Big game, small game, royal game, big game hunters, game preserve, etc.

The sunrises and sunsets in Africa are a testament to an ecstatic and kaleidoscopic rhythm of beginning and end. And all of it revolved around the obvious light of the sun by day and the more delicate truth of the moon by night. Animals, then, and the group mind-set among us travelers, were all in harmony. It was a miracle to behold.

Then something happened that put me more in touch with what I was capable of doing where injustice was concerned. Leopards were royal game in East Africa, which meant no one was allowed to shoot them. Some of the people on the safari wandered away from the trained hunters and spotted a leopard and her cubs in a tree. They raised their rifles and took aim. I couldn't help myself. I grabbed another rifle and turned it on the humans. I told them I would shoot them if they shot the leopard. They were so shocked and chagrined that I became persona non grata until I left the safari the next morning.

I think I really would have shot that man with a rifle turned on the leopard. So I ask myself: What does that say about me? I've thought about it for years. My anger at injustice has not diminished or changed as I move along my spiritual path. Since the "taking" of life is the highest cosmic and spiritual crime, where does that leave the human race in relation to how we conduct our affairs of state and human justice?

I'm Over Feeling I Need My Family Around Me at Thanksgiving and Christmas

The turkey and the pumpkin pie and Christmas cookies better be good, so as to supersede the salt on the wounds of the family history that's being dug up yet again. May the dialogue be salty and the outcome sugary just to avoid homicide.

I'm Not Over Making Money

I don't know that money is the root of *all* evil, but it can certainly deter the human being from attaining a spiritual balance.

My family never had more than $300 in the bank. I didn't know the value of money until I became an adult. And I wonder if I know the value of it even now.

Am I over the need for making money? No. I'm still interested in it because I want to be safe in the face of what could happen if we proceed along the course we've chosen. I have come to the decision that I will spend what money I make on the things I need to be self-sufficient. For example, I have installed wood-burning inserts in my fireplaces because they are more efficient for wood-fired heat. I need no other source of heat in the winter and I don't use any other form of energy (except solar) for heating.

I have a garden where I grow much of what I eat. I have a well that I drink out of. The water is pumped into my house via solar heating. I have solar heating for my hot water. I have a solar-powered freezer to keep the rest of the food I need. I will get some chickens when I feel the time is right. I have had my house inspected for mice, insects, cracks in the walls, fire hazards, etc., so I know it's in good shape. I use gas for cooking (again, it's solar powered). So I spend my money on these things that are necessary to be self-sufficient in life. I don't buy many clothes anymore. I have enough. I auction off my old clothing to benefit animal rescue organizations. I don't wear much jewelry except for my own Chakra jewelry line which helps balance the chakras (more on that later).

I travel coach on airplanes and buy a companion seat for Terry so she will be comfortable. I buy senior movie seats, and usually walk where I want to go. I have a housekeeper once a week. Otherwise I do all the cooking and cleaning myself. My needs are rather simple. The older I get, the more basic my life becomes, like a child's almost. It's those middle, creative, and productive years that so skew our values.

I think of money not in terms of how much there is in my bank account, but more in terms of why I need it in the first place. I like Thornton Wilder's quote in *The Matchmaker*: "Money is like manure. It should be spread around encouraging young things to grow."

I'm Over People Who Don't Know That We Are All Performing All the Time

They say there are only two businesses in the world—everyone else's business and show business. But then, we're *all* living a show of some kind . . . those in the business of show and those who are not. Even war and especially politics. "Shock and awe." "Mission accomplished." "Surge the troops." "Win one for the Gipper." It's all movie dialogue, and sometimes not even very good dialogue at that.

There are a few aspects of the life show we live that I think I'm over. I've always been a little surprised at how many people find show business so intriguing. "Were you really in love with your leading man?" "Was that real blood coming out of the wound?" "Can you turn it off at night after work?" Everyone wants to know about show business and glamour.

Even the people with the money who finance our "show"

are intrigued by how we do it. I think they are mesmerized at our ability to manipulate emotions and feelings. They manipulate business for money; we manipulate audiences for acknowledgment and to feel loved.

I used to watch politicians and other powerful people quake in the presence of Frank Sinatra, who knew exactly what was happening and played it for all it was worth. They may have snickered among themselves afterward, but they were never honest enough to try and exert their own power in the presence of a seriously talented human being . . . talented not only at singing and acting, but deeply talented at knowing what other people wanted. I loved to watch him in the presence of real gangsters, men who killed people when they wanted to. They might have felt they held the lives of others in their hands, but Frank *moved* the lives of others with his acting and singing. He employed the universal language of music to touch the hearts of killers and he knew it. So did they . . . even though, as I sometimes heard, a few of them wanted to "whack the canary" for being a "know-it-all."

Frank has a prominent position on my Walls of Life. My favorite picture is one of us singing together when I opened for him on his final tour. Of course we were old friends (he put me in *Some Came Running* and *Can-Can*) but even I felt somehow subservient to his presence and his talent. That didn't stop me, though, from standing in front of his monitor once in a while so he couldn't read his lyrics. We all knew he couldn't remember words much, so it was fun to watch him make them up. That was worth the price of admission for the audience, too.

How many times did I rush to catch the private plane after the show, my long, sequined gown stuck with sweat to my body, tripping in my high heels up the stairway of the plane because I knew he would simply take off as he stepped from his limo whether I was there or not. On board, he would childishly throw jelly beans or whatever else was available, turning the flight into a kind of crazy adult flying nursery school.

When he and Dean were together in front of an audience, it was their childhood dream of "watch me" come true. They were both comedic perfectionists, but Frank knew that Dean was the master. Sometimes he even liked to prove that to the audience. He would tell a short joke and get no reaction. Then he'd bring Dean forward to tell the same joke and watch as the audience convulsed with laughter. "Why didn't they think I was funny?" he'd ask Dean, and he meant it quite seriously. Dean would answer, "Because you're not," and the audience would convulse again.

I loved how honest they were with the audience. Yes, they were both superb singers, but the thrill for the people out front was how they related to each other with insults, teasing, and overall tomfoolery. They made jokes about their sex lives, their families, their work, and most certainly, the "Mob." The audience loved it because they knew that both of them were telling the truth. Sometimes they would get me up on the stage, urging me to join them with respect and gentle humor, and I always realized afterward that I had learned something more about comedy by being with them. They taught me that comedy wouldn't be funny unless it was based on truth.

I also learned later in my life that when telling the truth about the past, it is most definitely a question of perspective. My recollections are just that—mine. Somebody else who might have been present could see the "truth" in an entirely different light. For example, when in one of my books I wrote about Frank and Dean and the "Boys" (gangsters) and their association with the joints they played and the behavior I saw therein, Frank was upset. It didn't last long, but he thought I understood the oath of "omertà" which forbids the discussion of such matters upon the pain of death. I, of course, never took such an oath and frankly didn't even know what it was. But knowing and being around the "Boys" was part of my life and an important part at that. As an actor, observing their behavior and clocking the results was a kind of acting lesson for me. When Frank and his then-wife and his daughter denied he even knew them, I found that funnier than all his adolescent antics. What on earth did they think they were doing? The whole world knew Frank started singing in clubs owned by Mob guys. So of course there was an association. I had a hard time processing their public denials. To Frank, I had been such a part of his "in" life that he expected me somehow to know all the Hoboken rules and obey them—even though he certainly didn't.

Those of us in show business sometimes call people who are not in show business "civilians" because they don't understand what it takes to be loved by being "really" real. If we're good at it, we usually can make a civilian believe anything we want them to believe.

From the time we were very young, we non-civilians needed to be loved more than most. We needed to be acknowledged and noticed because we desperately felt we had something valuable to say. So with each of us non-civilian, creative, insecure, yet demandingly talented people there is a divalike environment around us charged with edgy ideas, which lead the civilians to water but never let them drink. We tease, cajole, propagandize, and promise to bring the heart and soul of the human to the screen or stage to be understood and related to. We think we understand the civilian world, but the truth is we gave that up long ago. At the same time we divas say we reflect the civilians back to themselves.

How can we still be one of them when we are profiting (and suffering from!) the vicissitudes of fame? Once we become famous there is only the memory of the struggle. We never want to be un-famous again.

My orientation has been somewhat different because I labored for so many years as a dancer. Dancers aren't as interested in fame as much as they are determined to be good team players. Dancers are not so caught up in our own identities except insofar as how it enables us to perform without getting hurt. Dancers are creative soldiers. If I were in a foxhole,

I'd want a dancer with me—they think fast, are survival-oriented, able to sacrifice themselves, and will save the team. Dancers are rarely divas (Nureyev excepting). I don't know why opera stars are divas; maybe it's something to do with their throats and cold air. Dancers will dance on top of snow in a blizzard if told it's necessary.

The reason I became a famous person—an individual—is because I was never a very good dancer. Bob Fosse used to say I was wrong about that—but then, he wasn't a very good dancer either. He and I were thinkers who moved around a lot. And if someone else did something good, we'd steal it and make it ours.

All of that is Broadway folklore now, but to me it is ever-present. The famous "Steam Heat" dance number choreographed by Bob Fosse has moves inspired by various MGM movie musicals, which Fosse may or may not have "borrowed" and then made into a classic all its own. It was (and is) performed in black tuxedos and black derbies. It usually gets a standing ovation.

So often I've tried to describe what it feels like to command a live audience from the stage. There's no feeling in the world that is more satisfying. And no feeling is more devastating than when it falls flat and bores the audience. Las Vegas was my best teacher when I was developing my one-woman show. It was simple. If I heard ice tinkling in glasses, I knew I was boring them.

Yes, we are all involved in the world where our ultimate

goal is to show truth. When a politician gives a magnificently moving speech, he is actually a consummate actor who had a consummate writer preparing his material, so squaring the circle of what moves and inspires humanity. It's the elements of show business that make a winner in politics.

I have, in my humble opinion, become something of a connoisseur of reality in my life because I've been privileged to experience so many points of view through traveling and my relationships with such a wide range of people. I'm usually right about the authenticity of a person's presentation of themselves. Show business is a cruel educator in that department. When I've worked with brilliant actors who seem so real when they act a part, I've come to realize that underneath they *are* real to themselves.

I'm Not Over Vanity,
But I'm Trying

Let's face it, vanity is as old as the hills. Entire civilizations are known to us today only because of how long-dead people looked, dressed, paraded, and even adorned themselves for death. Our museums are full of the stuff of their vanity. But what does vanity mean really? Does it revolve around how others see us or how we see ourselves?

When I was a teenager I was embarrassed by my red hair and freckles. And I had a tiny birthmark under my left arm, which today I hardly notice. But as young people we feel embarrassed by being seen as different in any way. We are inculcated with advertising propaganda as to what is acceptable and pretty.

As I've grown older, of course, I've dealt with a new set of vanity issues. I don't know if I would have been concerned in a different way if I hadn't been in show business. I honestly never cared how I looked or how I dressed until I was about fifty years old. I was a "character" in life and a character in films. My roles in films weren't dependent on beauty. I thought I was pretty enough once those freckles left my face around the age of 20. As a dancer, I exercised when I worked in a musical, and I thought that was enough. I ate anything I wanted and didn't put on weight. Of course, *weight* in those days was a healthy subject, not an unhealthy one.

I remember making *The Trouble with Harry* for Alfred Hitchcock. I had just come out of the chorus of *Pajama Game* on Broadway and was thin and broke. My diet as a chorus girl was Horn & Hardart's Automat food. I could live on ten cents a meal. There were lemons and sugar at the tables and water at the fountain. I'd make lemonade. Peanut butter and raisin bread sandwiches were ten cents in the food windows. So I had my peanut butter–raisin bread sandwich and lemonade for two nickels. A good diet, too.

Working with Hitch meant eating with him. On location for *Harry,* my breakfast was pancakes, fried eggs, fruit, toast, and jam. My lunch was worse because the desserts were heaven, and dinner was something I had to learn how to eat with him: meat, potatoes, appetizers, seven-course meals and Grand Marnier soufflés or the like to top it off. I never realized that my weight was visibly changing on film—maybe ten pounds from one scene to another when the film was assembled! The president of Paramount called me and asked me what I thought I was doing. I said, "Eating what I couldn't afford before." He said, "Now you've got some money, you're not going to starve. Quit or we'll have to shoot retakes." That hadn't occurred to me. Hitch obviously had a food problem. But with him, carrying extra weight *was* his image. I was a different story.

Because I had a high metabolism and moved around a lot, I had no real problem until I was about fifty. Then vanity became an issue. Until then, I hardly sat in the makeup chair. Frank Westmore (my makeup man) literally wrestled me to the floor on several occasions because his job was on the line if I didn't look pretty. I hated the creamy texture of the makeup, and the itch of the mascara, and *above all* the time I thought I was wasting sitting in the chair. My hairstyle was the result of a stage manager in *Me and Juliet* dunking my head in the chorus basement sink. I had long red hair that swished around on stage and drew attention away from the star, Isabel Bigley (which, truth be told, wasn't difficult). When he let me up for air, the stage manager chopped off my ponytail and pushed me back onstage. The bowl cut has been my style ever since. I was not very imaginative, and hairstyles took too much time. Besides, my pixie cut worked well when dancing Bob Fosse's hat routines.

Soon after coming to Hollywood, I realized that wigs were the way to go, not only when playing parts on screen but also in life, because I never had to sit with curlers under the dryer. That saved time in the makeup chair too. The hairdresser did all the work when I wasn't there. But when my middle fifties came around, I began to notice that I was getting a lot of grandmother-part offers. I didn't see myself that way at all. What was happening? I was, in my own mind, still young, bouncy, an invisible guerrilla traveler, a kid. Wrong. After some hard thought, I had my face lifted. Never do that in the middle of a love affair because it's disconcerting to your partner. And forget about having sex during recovery time. That's the best way to pop your stitches.

But I must say I loved how I looked afterward. In fact, I became quite enamored with my face and preferred to have dinner wherever there were mirrors. Which brings me to the next show business necessity in real life.

I Will Never Get Over
Good Lighting

First of all, you need to know where to sit. If it's daytime, you sit *facing* the outside light. Natural light is very nice for the skin—as long as it's not direct sunlight. If you're really smart, you place your partner just to the side of where the light is hitting you. You'll know you are in the right daytime lighting position when you can't see his face. He is completely backlit. You won't know how he is reacting to your daytime dialogue, but you *do* know you look as good as possible when the sun is out.

At night, choose a restaurant with candlelit tables. Even ask for another candle. Claim you can't see the menu. *Never* sit where there is an overhead light. It makes you look like Grandma Moses. And *never* sit where you can feel a cross-light splash across your face. A two-year-old looks haggard in that condition. If you are a person who is stopped on the street for a "reality" interview, ask them what filter they have in the camera. Black full pro mist is the best, but everything else will look slightly blurred, which is what you want for your face. Otherwise, just keep walking.

I have no solution for the paparazzi who jump out at you in highly inappropriate environments. Except perhaps murder. But then, even paparazzi can be reincarnated.

When you are doing a TV interview, remember to tell the camera people you want the camera high and the key light low. They will hate you for knowing what you're doing, but insist, even if you turn into a diva. It's easier for me nowadays because I'm so old they think I *must* be an expert. In fact, Marlene Dietrich taught me how to light myself when we made *80 Days*. She was the master of lighting, as well as the master of costume fittings. I used to sit and watch her being fitted in everything from leather tuxedos to full-length sequined gowns. Her fittings lasted for six hours. She was literally the last one left standing. She would ponder deeply over exactly how close the sequins should be sewn together. She loved to design the sequins so the audience could just see through them, revealing the shape of her legs. She taught me a new use for 2½ millimeter pearls. (They were to be put in the center of my bra so you would think they were my nipples.) She also showed me how to string a small, nearly invisible chain under my chin which was then attached to pincurls on either side of my face. This was the Dietrich face-lift. Of course I had a headache by lunch, but it was worth it. She ate only every other day, and not much even then. That's how she kept her figure. Not something I could ever do.

She was having a love affair with Mike Todd on *80 Days* until I introduced him to Elizabeth Taylor. Marlene was good about it. She remembered that Mike had tossed out Evelyn Keyes for her anyway.

I loved to overhear the negotiations for diamonds and rubies between Mike and Elizabeth just to get her to go out to dinner. Elizabeth was no fool and Mike was no cheapskate. I sometimes wondered what a roll in the hay would cost. Elizabeth used to come to my one-room apartment in Malibu and tell me that Mike seduced her as a snake would seduce a mongoose. Every man I ever introduced her to fell in love with her. She saw to that. One of them purposely nearly ran his car off a Malibu cliff out of longing for her.

I had a darling boxer dog at the time, and whenever we came back to my place and the dog had pooped on the floor, she would clean it up, protesting that she wanted a simpler life. She was and is a very down-to-earth person—a woman I adore completely, a loyal and funny friend.

I learned a great lesson in lighting from her one night. Mike had recently died in that tragic plane crash, and Elizabeth had taken up with Eddie Fisher. The town and it seemed the entire country was upset with her for stealing Eddie from Debbie *and* for doing it so soon after Mike's death. There was a party at her agent's house. She asked me to come and sit with her at a small table, which happened to be situated next to a candle-lit patio. She was drinking champagne from a sparkling crystal glass. Very subtly, she positioned herself in between me and the outside candles (they always work). She began to quietly talk about her love for Mike and why Eddie meant so much to her because of his relationship with Mike. Her eyes welled up with violet tears as she held her sparkling crystal glass close to her face. When the tears were about to fall, she subtly moved her champagne glass just under her eyes. I'll never forget it. Her tears splashed like diamonds into the champagne as she talked about missing Mike so much. I'd never seen anything more beautiful or moving, and the entire party seemed to pause in wonder for a moment. It all worked because her words were true and because she used her extensive experience in front of the camera to accentuate her emotions. She is a great lady and the personification that All Life Is Show Business.

I have come to the point in my life that I would rather just play a great character than worry so much how I look while I'm doing it. I'm not completely over my vanity, but the part that I *am* over is a relief.

I'm Over Antibiotics Unless I'm Dying

I've had sinus infections all my life. Over the years, the doctors gave me every antibiotic they could think of. They would work for a while, but the infections always came back. Then, about five years ago, I got very sick. A drip from my nose caused spasmodic coughing fits so intense that it put me in the emergency room three times. None of my doctors could pinpoint what was wrong. So I took more antibiotics. Nothing worked.

Then one day I asked for a CT scan of my sinuses. The result was shocking: the entire right side of my face was full of pus. Long story short, I decided to have sinus surgery in L.A. The team got me prepared for surgery . . . at least that's what I was told they were doing. The preparation consisted mostly of the anesthesiologist and nurses asking me about movies and Hollywood. They seemed disorganized to me.

One of the drugs they were pumping into my arm was supposed to dry up all my mucus and spit. I had a severe coughing fit and I was unable speak. The surgeon thought I was sedated and other doctors came in and took tests. They pronounced me in good health. I was awake, but still couldn't speak. The surgeon held a long, long tube up over his head like a circus performer about to do a trick. Then he proceeded to put the long tube into my nose and push it down and inside my face. It was excruciating. I tried to speak, but couldn't. I had heard stories about people whom doctors thought were under anesthesia when they really weren't. It was happening to me!

I grabbed the long tube and pulled it out of my nose and sat up. I somehow got off the table and managed to croak, "I'm out of here. Where are my shoes?"

I heard one of the anesthesiologists say that the drug I had been given produced a fight-or-flight response if the patient wasn't out. Fight-or-flight described me perfectly, all right. Probably due to my status as a celebrity, the nurses found my clothes and shoes pronto. I still couldn't speak very well. I became a one-person escape artist and no one stopped me. I don't remember calling a cab, but one came and I went home.

I will never go to that hospital or see those doctors again.

A few weeks later, I had the sinus operation in Santa Fe as outpatient surgery. It went well. The doctors told me they had never seen such an infected backup of pus, the sickly stench of which permeated the surgery room. The rehab from the surgery was difficult, but I have been fine ever since.

My question is: why didn't someone suggest a CT scan five

years before? The doctors assumed my problem was allergies, and they said I must be allergic to my dog. They were right about allergies, but not about Terry, yet they just kept giving me antibiotics instead of treating the actual allergies.

After my surgery, my homeopath intervened and gave me a homeopathic regimen. I drained for one entire month, and that was the end of my allergies. The main remedy was allium cepa, which I would recommend for allergies. I religiously keep my homeopathic remedies with me, and now I am fine.

Homeopathic medicines work because everything in the world has a frequency at which it gives off energy—you can actually measure it. The homeopath produces a medicine that vibrates at the same frequency as the thing you are allergic to, which cancels it out and results in remarkable healing. They work particularly well for me, I think, because I am sensitive to the frequencies which obey the law of similars. Some skeptics will say it's all in my head, a "placebo effect," but I promise you that homeopathy works better for me than any pharmaceuticals. And certainly better than surgeons who are proud they have celebrity clientele. As far as I've seen, celebrities get the worst treatment there is from the medical profession.

As a Sometime Asthmatic, I Am Over Deep Breathing

I have found a cure for asthma. It's called the ButeyKo Technique, which is a set of breathing techniques. This is how it works:

Step I: The "Control Pause" Breathing Test
Take two normal breaths, then breathe out, and then see how long you can hold your breath. The goal is to be able to hold it for at least 60 seconds.

Step II: Shallow Breathing
Take shallow breaths using only your nose for five minutes. Keep your mouth shut. Then take the "control pause" test again to see if your count has improved. Hint: If your nose is blocked up, pinch your nostrils together for a few minutes. This helps clear the nasal passages.

Step III: Putting It Together

Repeat the "test-breathe-test" routine four or five times in a row. It will take about 25 minutes in total. Repeat this training session three or four times a day for a week. Don't worry if you miss a session or two, just carry on. The goal is increasing your "control pause" test result.

There it is. It's that simple. After a week you should be able to breathe out and hold your breath for a count of over 60 seconds. Your asthma will be much better. It also helps prevent heart attacks because you are controlling the amount of carbon dioxide in your system.

I Am Over Being Polite
to Boring People

I am not good at "smalk." That's small talk. I try to maintain my patience, but it abandons me completely and I try not to tell the smalker what I'm thinking. I try to walk away, but if I can't, I stand and listen for an inordinate amount of time, blinking and nodding. They go on and on, and I nod and blink on and on in return. The trick is to never speak or answer them or acknowledge what they are saying in any way. Finally, if they won't stop talking, I go into a trance and meditate. At least that way I don't hurt their feelings and can practice patience on another planet.

I don't know why so many people have gone rusty on thinking. Perhaps it was the dumbing-down of the W years. Or perhaps too many people are living most of their days on their computers and thus have the mind-set that the computer thinks for them. To have a thought-provoking conversation with someone is more difficult than pushing a square peg into a round hole . . . or hanging soap bubbles on a clothesline. There is no focus and no real curiosity in too many people. Yes, I'm over being a chatterer or the one being chattered at.

I'm Over Trusting the FDA

I'm over trusting the FDA if they ban the sale and manufacture of injectable vitamin C containing injectable magnesium chloride and injectable vitamin B-complex 100. These two substances are routinely added to intravenous C to make the "Meyers Cocktail" used for conditions such as chronic fatigue syndrome, hepatitis, AIDS, mononucleosis, and flu.

Why is the FDA doing this? Because vitamin C and magnesium and vitamin B complex can't be patented and therefore won't be taken through the standard FDA approval process. The approval process would have to be funded privately, which could cost billions. We need to have a choice of treatment that is not ruled by Big Pharma.

Ageing in Hollywood?!
Get Over It

It's good to have some modicum of self-awareness when one is faced with the reality of ageing in Hollywood. At least it makes it less lonely because you become more and more acquainted with your real long-time companion—yourself.

So often I've wondered how I would define my identity if I weren't a so-called icon, a Hollywood star of yesteryear (and sometimes now), a person whose image has been watched and whose words have been read by a shockingly great number of people. Take away all that, and who am I?

I've seriously thought about this, and finally I realized that no actress ever really leaves Hollywood unless she finds God and gives up everything else. I've come close, but no cigar. Hollywood stars really are our American version of royalty, I suppose. Hollywood changes your DNA. You believe your own publicity. You are catered to in every possible way. You become publicly insecure because you want the public to love you, yet most of the time a successful star doesn't feel he or she deserves that adoration. Success is not a panacea for needing to be loved. In so many ways, it is a surefire way to avoid the issue of self-love. Do we deserve love from others when we don't even love ourselves?

The money, the adoration, the power over others—it's all ridiculous. The abuse of artistic freedom is scandalous. The unreal fantasy of it all renders you borderline schizophrenic. And when you get older and the phone stops ringing and you essentially are respected simply for having survived your long haul; when you are happy to do character parts as an extra added attraction in otherwise lackluster films, then you look back over the well-produced phantasmagoria of it all and ask yourself, "Did I behave reasonably well? Did I abuse my power? Did I keep many people waiting? Did I do it for money, for love, for my own personal growth, and to express my own identity?"

My answer to these questions would be: I couldn't *not* live a life of self-expression. That's probably due to the repression of my middle-class childhood, which ignited in me the need to become different from those other folks down the block. Also, on some level, I knew I was fulfilling the thwarted dreams of both my parents. So does it all come down to family in the final analysis? Do we want to avoid living in the self-denying world that squelched our parents' dreams?

The real artists in Hollywoodland dare to explore their fathomless pasts in order to keep looking for who they are.

Their frustration, neuroses, and bad behavior are linked directly to deep, deep insecurities, and if they can miraculously touch on a childhood terror that up to now they've conveniently covered up, they more than likely will produce a small or monumental masterpiece of art.

Being involved in other people's lives is exhausting when you're in the twilight throes of figuring out your own life. I want to be as clear as I can about my own past and what I want for my future life. I would love to continue to act. It is fun for me and I still love to explore the eccentricity of human beings. I like the familial environment on a film set. I do not like getting up so early in order to shoot by the light of the sun, and I hate the traffic in LA. But I really enjoy the makeup trailer, where all the gossip and inner workings of the film you're shooting are shared and dissected. I enjoy the craft service table, laden with donuts, snacks, and all manner of treats that soothe your insecurities between takes.

I don't, and probably never did, feel all that insecure about anything much. I don't know why not. I've not been good in some movies, but I was satisfied with knowing I had worked hard. As my agent said once, "If what you've done doesn't work, not that many people will see it anyway."

An actor's relationship with his or her agent is a primary one. There are many jokes made about not being able to get your agent on the phone, or about how you go out and get a job for yourself and your agent collects 10 percent. I admit if I have trouble reaching someone on the phone, it is a real problem.

But that goes for anybody who doesn't call me back right away.

I don't do email. I refuse. I want to hear the tenor of the voice and the spaces in between the words of the person I'm talking to. If I did email, I'd be living in a computer world. I like *real* world contact.

How agents with a big roster of clients keep all the projects and castings correct is beyond me. It's a particular talent for compartmentalization, something akin to what a really good worker behind the counter at Starbucks has. Each of the agent's clients feels he or she is the only one. We expect the agent to remember each and every detail of our careers as though they'd stewed over these elements like we do. We know the agents play the clients off against each other. We know they'd like each project to be a package deal where only the agency's clients are involved. Even though show business is really the "Big Knife," most of our business is run on the strength of personal relationships. People remember each other, for good and for ill. That's one reason no one ever really wants to tell you the truth. It will come back to haunt you either in revenge, or in future profit and thanks. I have an agent who tells me the truth. Jack Gilardi is personally interested in my continuing to work, which isn't easy when you are looking for material for a woman my age. We talk every day even if it's just about things happening out in the world. Jack loves to tease me. He stands about five feet six inches, but he tells everyone he used to be six foot five before working with me. Sometime when we are discussing possible future parts for me, he calls them "roles for old ladies." He catches himself and rephrases, saying they are looking for "women with maturity." I believe he deals with me in truth, just as I do with him. But that's not typical in Hollywood. Come to think of it, he's my fourth Jack!

This lack of truth telling has been difficult for me in my twilight years. I see no reason not to tell the truth. It will all become evident at some time later anyway. Truth telling is somehow politically incorrect. Maybe it's because there's less time left for me in this life, but I'm innately compelled to tell someone if they are full of crap and not waste any more time about it. Time is ticking away. And *timing* is everything.

I feel that I will go on to make many more films. A friend tells me I'm going for the record of old-age working. How peaceful it is not to have to look particularly pretty anymore or to wear a size 6. I am concerned about my weight, but more because of cholesterol and insulin problems than vanity. As long as there is a good Pro-mist filter on the camera and a few chimera lights around, I know I'll be all right. I'm glad the union requires the studio to provide a driver for actors when we're working, because in the morning I'm no good at it, and it's dangerous for me to drive at night now.

I like watching the parade of new stars. I place bets with friends as to how long each will be around. (Not nice of us, I know.) So much of longevity has nothing to do with looks or talent. It's something indefinable—like star power. How do you define that? You know it when you see it. I never thought much about how long I would last. I'm like an animal in that respect. I live in the moment. However, one of my problems in life is that I'm ten years ahead of the curve on matters of spiritual science and self-exploration. In social settings, I continually have to work to keep my conversation simple and my investigations a personal matter.

People identify with other people; they don't identify with subjects and information unless it relates to them. I have learned this through the publication of my various books. In the beginning of my spiritual questing and wanderings, people identified with me much more than they did after I'd found some answers. When I got specific and began to share the underpinnings of spiritual science (the energy of the chakras, vibrational frequency of healing techniques, principles of karma and reincarnation, and the facts about extraterrestrial presence), it got to be too dense for a lot of people. If I stayed with my own journey as a human being trying to figure out who I was, they could identify. Being an entertainer didn't help. I remember once a journalist from San Francisco said, "How can we take your spiritual teachings seriously when you wear sequins on the stage?" It took me aback. (Aback so far I still haven't recovered!) What does my wardrobe have to do with it?

Then I thought about it. When you're an actor, a performer, or anybody who knows how to make fiction seem real, you are suspect. When I asked that journalist if he thought I should wear a monk's robe and make myself ugly in order to be taken more seriously in spiritual matters, he nodded yes. I know that says more about him than me, but there is a "knowing" comment in there somewhere. It's got to do with my favorite subject—*reality*. What is it? How do we know if something or someone or some event is real or not? Since reality itself is a matter of perception, how can anyone define one view of reality as a consensus for all? So I'm back to the journey of my own perceptions. How *I* see something is how that thing is authentic to *me*.

I learned after many years in show business that if an expressive artist shares his or her point of view as authentically as possible, it will somehow be identifiable to large masses of people.

I'm Over Being Under a Big Corporate Conglomerate's Control

So often now I hear a great filmmaker say, "Could we get such and such a film financed today?" No. The answer is always no because the days of old Hollywood moguls who were visionaries, who were eccentrically stubborn and in love with celluloid, are gone. Jack Warner, Hal Wallis, Sol Siegel, and Lew Wasserman must be looking down and weeping for their beloved industry of fantasy and passion. Marketing departments run the industry and it's all about money now. It's no longer about passionate self-expression that mirrors humanity back to itself. The good scripts are not at the studios anymore because the development process destroys any original idea. Minor executives and people who should be bankers make copious notes on every screenplay, which is then delivered to the writer, who is ordered to make changes. Because he wants to get his picture made, he agrees. Hence you have studio movies totally unlike the great ones of yesterday.

Tent-pole pictures (the franchise pictures full of special effects and moving, swirling objects) don't need to have a plot that works or even makes sense. Studio people seem to have forgotten that having a first, second, and third act is a good structure. They also play to the most dumbed-down members of the audience nowadays. People are so stressed out economically and in their individual lives that they just want to be blindly entertained in a manner that doesn't make them have to think. Studio pictures are not an artistic contribution from and to our nation anymore. They play into our insecurities and our character defects out of a desire for nothing but profit. That's because most of the studios are now owned by big corporations. Corporations care about profit more than quality, and it costs about the same to market and distribute a big picture as it does a small one. So if a studio puts aside $300 million for making movies, they would rather do three big ones than twenty small ones of quality. It saves money.

I've had many studio producers tell me they make horror films and other fare that induces fear in the audience's mind because the lives of audience members are so negative they need to be entertained by something more frightening than their own experience. Is that really a good reason to make a movie? Good scripts are turned down all the time because they might make the audience think too much!

Every star in Hollywoodland has a dollar figure by his or

her name. That's the amount each person is considered to be worth at the box office. With those dollar figures acting as a price tag, presales of a film are solicited overseas. Each star is worth so much money in Germany, Brazil, South Africa, Japan, etc. It has nothing to do with the star's talent or the quality of the film being shopped. Based on the box office worth of the stars attached to the film, the film distributors overseas then determine what they will pay to distribute it in their market. The total budget of each film is determined by these pre-sales. I know that I can get more money added to the budget if I'm in a comedy or a musical. Thus, I become typecast if I only listen to the presales definition of what I'm worth. Surprise is eliminated from the formula, because off-beat casting is simply not recognized by the money men.

There is a deep and sincere underdog respect for filmmakers who make pictures like *Slumdog Millionaire, Little Miss Sunshine, The Hurt Locker, The Kids Are All Right,* and all those independent films that have budgets next to nothing but are driven by the belief and vision of the filmmaker, who sometimes hocks his home to keep the filming going. The studios don't like to take risks anymore, but they aren't alone in that. They seem to be reflecting the fear experienced everywhere in the business community of this country these days.

I've talked to so many distraught writers who have been forced to compromise their original scripts. Studio employees who justify their jobs by making their notes often ruin the authenticity of the piece. The horror of it is that sooner or later the writer will not only compromise but will feel "Oh, it's not really that bad." But it *is* that bad.

In the old days the studio heads either liked a script or not. Sometimes they would have a note or two, but the writers always knew they could humor them and walk away.

We've been suffering badly in Hollywood for a few years now. People who work "below the line" (technicians, grips, drivers, caterers, cleaning establishment owners, etc.) are going into foreclosure with their homes because hardly any films are being made. Our business is in Big Trouble. It's so disappointing. Spirit is what fuels the art of making films. Now spirit has been replaced with budget cuts and market sheets. I look back with longing at how it used to be. Those old moguls who ran, ruined, and inspired our lives don't seem so bad now.

One of my disappointments with young people I know in film is that they don't ask me enough serious questions. They should pick my brain about Mike Todd, Hal Wallis, the Warner brothers, Wilder, Wyler, Fosse, Nichols, Hitchcock, etc. They are too focused on the red carpet if they're actresses, how to seem dangerous and sexy if they're actors, and how to manipulate everyone else if they're directors. If I were an up-and-comer sitting with me, I'd put aside all decorum and smother me with questions.

I can always tell how serious a filmmaker is by how much he knows about the history of Hollywood. Does he or she have any idea about the struggles involved with making the hundred or so greatest films of all time? When we are young, it's often hard to think of anything but what is happening right in front of or around us. But the true artist can see beyond this limited (and limiting) viewpoint. A great artist, I believe, lives in the past, present, and future all at the same time. That's one difference between a great artist and a talented craftsman.

I Am Over Driving at Night
Unless It's a Really Short Trip

Leaving my car in the garage after the sun goes down has been difficult because I like to be in charge of my nights as well as my days.

I eat out with friends a lot and that usually happens at night. Sometimes they pick me up, but I don't like to impose on them. So I usually suggest an early dinnertime so I can come and go while it's still light. I plead easier parking in daylight.

Pretty soon I'll have to give up driving altogether. That's when I will hire a combination driver, cook, pilot, and well-intentioned friend. Hopefully that private plane will come before too long!

Get Over Thinking
You're Just One Person

Probably one of the reasons why reincarnation makes sense to me is because I understand how each one of us is so many people. When we open up and allow our soul's memory to emerge and express itself, we can be amazed at the talent for multiple personalities we each have. I don't mean multiple personalities in the sense of a psychological disorder. I mean each of us has had multiple experiences in past lifetimes that equip our souls with memories and intuitions that can't be explained any other way. How did I know and recognize streets and temples when I first went to India? Why did I find myself speaking Portuguese when I was in Brazil? Each human being can point to any number of similar experiences, specific moments that make them wonder why and how they know what they know.

Of course, reincarnation is an accepted fact in a large part of the world, particularly in those that were home to the most ancient civilizations (India, Tibet, the Himalayas, China).

Most of those areas of the world have not been influenced or taught or programmed by Christianity.

Even Christian doctrine was not always in opposition to reincarnation, that is until the sixth century AD when Empress Theodora of Byzantium arranged an ecumenical council in Constantinople in the year 553. The Pope himself and many bishops boycotted the meeting because Theodora was planning an eradication of the understanding of soul reembodiment in the Gospels, replacing the idea of reincarnation with that of resurrection. The Greek philosopher Origen taught physical reembodiment in ancient days and, according to many experts, so did Jesus of Nazareth when teaching his disciples. "And who do you say I am?" he asked his disciples in Matthew 16: 15–16. He alluded to the truth that he had been Elias or Elijah previously. There are schools of spiritual study that understand the transfiguration to have been the enactment of several of Jesus's incarnations—including Adam, Moses, Abraham, Joseph, and even Noah.

When one understands karma, reincarnation—physical reembodiment of the soul—is paramount. "What the soul sows, so shall it reap." This means that every human soul is in control of his or her destiny, depending on what each human needs to work on the next time around. The soul lives on and the learning of self continues.

Empress Theodora was apparently a fascistic ruler of the first order. She and her husband, Emperor Justinian, wanted to control the destiny of their populace. She had her own intelligence organization and deployed it with great power and cruelty. Gore Vidal once wrote a script about her and educated me about her intentions as empress. She didn't like the idea of people being responsible for their own destiny. That was to be *her* role. So she arranged to stack the deck of attendees at the Ecumenical Council in order to strike any and all references to physical reembodiment from the Bible. Sadly, she was successful.

Having traveled so extensively in India and the Himalayas and Asia, I was more conversant with these points of view than my scientific-minded Christian friends in the West. What they could prove they would believe, but not otherwise.

When I first began writing in the sixties about having lived before, I was way ahead of the Western curve. Those people who had ventured into these areas of thought were with me, but I infuriated many others who thought it was loopy and I was the object of a fair amount of ridicule. Happily, that disdain has dissipated in the last thirty years as people have caught up with the possibility that reincarnation might be logical. Most of the ridicule didn't bother me, except for those film and theater critics who loved to review me playing a part as though it was one from a past life I should have turned down. I wondered if they accepted the Dalai Lama's lessons on physical reembodiment because he wore the correct wardrobe. And today I wonder if the same people who flock to so many yoga classes are those who previously believed I was nuts.

Many acting teachers today use meditation exercises to

encourage student actors to touch a past life experience which might help them play a part they are afraid of. I learned long ago that living *is* acting, and it always has been. Every day we choose what script we will write for ourselves, how we will play our part, what wardrobe we will wear, and what emotions we will allow ourselves to feel or to repress. I don't know whether I chose acting or acting chose me in this life. Either way, I am the writer, producer, wardrobe mistress, star, and director of my own play every day that I live. And I now know I have been ever since my soul came into being. My search these days is more about the soul. For example, when *did* it come into being? Was that the Big Bang?

I hear about twin souls and soul mates all the time. What is the difference? In my studies I've come to learn that soul mates (and everyone has a soul mate) are those souls that vibrate on exactly the same frequency. No other souls in the cosmos vibrate to the same frequency as ours and that of our soul mate. If we find our soul mate in this life, it can be quite difficult because it is like living with a double of ourselves. Since very few of us are happy with who we are, we see a constant reflection of that dissatisfaction in our soul mate. The trick would be to find a twin soul, which is a soul with whom we've had multiple incarnations, and have thus come to an understanding of who we are with them. I think people confuse their soul mate with a twin soul. I'm not sure I want to know my soul mate yet. I'm not ready, and I don't want to be miserable because of my inability to understand another person's issues because I have the same issues myself! I've learned a lot about who I am, but not enough to tolerate my soul mate.

From what I've learned, we don't necessarily incarnate with our soul mate at the same time, although I've met quite a few people who feel one of their children is their soul mate. It must be a beautiful experience if you come across one whom you believe is your soul mate and it works. But I would say that usually that person is actually a twin soul, not a soul mate.

So many people look for their soul mate to fall in love with and marry. I've found a much more contented way to live. I live alone and independently. My husband died years ago, and my adventures in sexual passion and romantic love have receded. Sometimes I look back and wonder what the hell I was doing with all those lovers. Was it meant to be, necessary, and growth-producing? Yes, I think so, but my life now, without the Sturm und Drang of passion, is much more pleasant. In fact, I've always found that friendship without sexual passion is much more healthy and lasting. When women my age say they need to find a man, I tell them to get a dog. There's no more loving and satisfying way to live than if you are content with yourself and your freedom.

The price of freedom is sometimes loneliness. We all know that. But how many of us have found loneliness *with* someone? That's the real sadness.

I, for one, revel in everything my lovers have taught me. But I'm glad they are out of my life and I'm left with real friends.

I'm very fortunate to have about seven real friends in my life. I know I can count on them for anything. And they can count on me. I think I know how to be a friend to another person because I'm a pretty good friend to myself. None of these seven friends lives or works in Hollywood. Hollywood is not the most conducive place to develop friendships. On the other hand, I've found it to be my most thorough teacher.

I Am Over the Gallows of Fame

Everyone, it seems, wants their fifteen minutes (at least!) of fame and seems to be ready to do anything to get it. At my age, I'm relieved that I never received all that much tabloid attention. I never wanted it. The loss of privacy was a price I wasn't willing to pay. When I watch Jennifer Aniston or Britney Spears go through their personal hells in public for the gratification of the tabloids, it turns my stomach. I know young people who would do anything to have that kind of time in the sun. What are they thinking? I know young people who would give up anything to be "a star." They don't even recognize they need to have some kind of talent first. They don't care. They don't care if they are publicly humiliated because of their lack of talent. I can't understand what "fame" means to them—or why it means so much.

Fame is a drug, a drug of annihilation. Why do so many

people want to be famous when they see how it can destroy your life?

Tabloid journalism is the opiate of the people these days. Everyone seems to want to partake of the salacious dramas splashed across their pages, personal tragedies and mistakes and conflicts that were never meant to be made public. The lives of the famous make money for everybody. The price of fame is the resulting isolation of the soul and the abdication of reality. Fame is not real. It is a fifteen-minute illusion. Famous people often cannot see the reality because they are blinded by the glare of the attention.

People in show business sometimes call everyone else a civilian, and we desperately want to know what the civilians want. What will they pay for? What can we do to make them pay even more attention to us? How can we wrestle the love from them that we never felt we had in our own lives? We know that the relation between us and these civilians is tenuous and at the same time symbiotic. We understand that we wouldn't be famous if it weren't for them. We want to know them (the civilians) and want to be adored by them, but we want to hang on to our throne of fame one more day, or decade, or lifetime, because we never again want to be like them—*not* famous.

We may go home and visit what we used to be, but we are profoundly grateful we are not one of them anymore. We don't want to talk about ourselves when we go back home because we know they will not understand. That's why we call them civilians. We notice that they love to dissect the details of our fame and fortune; that's what we represent for them, and we feel used. We know that they know where we came from. And we probably haven't figured out how our fame happened; we feel guilty and undeserving.

I sometimes watch the reality television show *Toddlers and Tiaras* and cringe at the sight of mothers forcing their daughters to live out their own thwarted desires to be the girl in the spotlight. The spotlight can blind a person. It can sentence you to a life of emotional isolation in its glare. It can make you drop your hat!

So much of the life a famous person lives is pretense. We think we need to look or seem a certain way. Perhaps the biggest negative of fame is what often happens to the children of the famous. They grow up as elitists and in general feel they are entitled to special treatment even though they themselves have done nothing to earn it.

Fame is a false god. Talent and hard work are not.

Again, there are only two businesses on the planet—show business and everyone else's business. Hollywood is show business perfected and made absolute. It feeds the designers, the food merchants, the hair coiffeurs, the car services, the musicians, the carpenters, the TV channels, the gossipers, the legitimate papers, the airlines, the hotels, the booze industry, the manicure salons, the makeup artists, the tuxedo mannequins, the exercise gyms, the diet gurus, the security agencies, the real estate market . . . and last but not least, it serves the hunger that civilians have for observing, criticizing, and sometimes even appreciating those who are the merchants of dreams, the purveyors of scandal, and the reflectors of many truths about our human condition.

Even world leaders are seduced by the Dream Factory, because they know (even if only subconsciously) that they are in show business, too. They would rather be famous than anything. They want to learn how to command attention and be adored. What gives some of them such lasting power? they wonder. How does somebody make a comeback stick? The guys who made the camera a means of communication realized pretty quickly that they had the key to all power . . . something like the internet today, but infinitely more able to be controlled and manipulated.

Sitting on the inside of fame looking out, I want to share with you just how insecure our position of power actually feels to us. Every famous person, if he or she is being remotely honest, feels today could be his or her last in the spotlight. We know that our "glamour" is tenuous and completely dependent upon the thoughts and opinions of all those civilians. Yes, we understand that we wouldn't be doing what we do without them. They are our lifeblood and our future.

We desperately need to understand what the civilians want while we are profoundly grateful we are not one of them anymore. Altogether the underpinnings of our Dream Factory are to be disguised at any cost because our little world of privilege is built on sand. It can blow away and disappear at any time.

When we act characters, we try to *be* a civilian, but at the end of the day we must come back to who we are—or who we are not. So, we need to do as much research on ourselves as we do on our characters. Therein lies the rub. Are we willing to soul search ourselves so that when emotional or material hard times come we are equipped with the kind of self-knowledge that will see us through? Self-searching while you're on top is a non sequitur, a contradiction, an unnecessary endeavor, and sometimes even a killjoy. We are told to be happy for what we have—enjoy it because it may not last long. We are not equipped to comprehend how we became successful in the first place, particularly if it happens quickly. We have a kind of "why me?" guilt, like the survivor of a natural disaster. Those who have spent years struggling to no avail are usually quite bitter when success and fame finally come to them, because they find they are just as miserable as they were before.

So many people I've observed don't allow themselves to accept their own success and good fortune. They look the gift horse in the mouth, and because of the fear that success will go away they feel constant neurosis and glamorous misery are the requisite conditions for being "good at their craft."

I may not be much of an artist; I'm probably good at my craft. But I am happy with what has happened in my life and, frankly, always have been. Even during the period preceding one of my comebacks, I was enjoying the world, even though no one cared much whether I was in or out or up or down. I never socialized much with the Hollywood crowd. I was usually off on a trip or following the call of a new love affair. Fame and success took a backseat to love and travel.

Now I do both inside myself.

When you understand why you are struggling to be noticed, the fame game is winnable. Otherwise, please, you should fear to go where angels do not tread. Stay un-famous and be less of a prisoner of other people's opinions and whims. Stay un-famous and be less neurotic. Stay un-famous and learn to know yourself in quietude. That state of being lasts longer than fame anyway, and at much less cost.

I Am Not Over
Good Journalists

To me there is nothing better than a persistent truth-seeking journalist. I agree with my Founding Fathers: great reporters and journalists are more important than government.

Over the years, I have truly enjoyed being questioned skeptically by my favorite, Mike Wallace. He was fair and tough. He was neither left- nor right-leaning. And he was fun, particularly if you understood that an ambush was most certainly in progress. I would like to have ambushed him right into my boudoir, but he knew better.

I liked Jack Newfield. He was hell-bent on keeping them honest. I'm sorry he's gone.

Pete Hamill was another favorite of mine, and one I had the pleasure of living with for a few years. He has now become a great writer about his favorite mistress of all: New York City.

To me, one of the best talk show interviewers was David Frost. He had the knack of going to your heart. He wasn't trying to entertain as some of the others do. He was genuinely interested in his subjects. You can see it all re-created in *Frost/ Nixon*.

Barbara Walters, whom I like very much, can make any-body cry. She did it to me. She says she doesn't know why she has that talent. I think it's because she's a fair female, the good friend we've always wanted to keep us balanced. She tells me she has stopped going to parties and gatherings. I know how she feels. Celebrities give the impression that they are everywhere all the time. A few, like me and Barbara, have wised up.

I never was one to gallivant around in order to be seen. I was much more interested in *looking*. These days, to get me to go to almost any event would take mountain moving. Besides, it's mostly about "smalking" anyway. I am appalled at the number of people who are famous for doing absolutely noth-ing but being seen at parties.

How can someone become famous for nothing? The time and money required for getting "dolled up" and being in fashion is outrageous. Have that many people been deprived of love and acknowledgment in their childhoods?

I was never interested in fashion. I was interested in com-fort. The two are antithetical. I was on the worst-dressed list for twenty-five years and didn't give a damn. Now I'm a senior who wears Chanel because I played Coco in a film and they give me the clothes for free. But even in Chanel, I skip the red carpet.

My relationship with celebrity isn't like that of most other well-known people. I am more often than not embarrassed by the attention of strangers, and adoration truly upsets me. When I conducted my spiritual seminars in the 80s, I realized that people were giving me too much credit for their progress in self-awareness. I just lit the flame . . . they saw to it that the flame burned with their own personal truth. Finally, I quit giving seminars, realizing that each person was his or her own best teacher.

My personal relationships with journalists have been fulfilling because they don't believe everything they're told and they continually ask questions for clarification. If they are good journalists, they usually have a cynical sense of humor. That appealed to me greatly because I love to laugh at the absurdity of most everything. I particularly liked calling them on their own sense of truth and objectivity as they reported what they saw. I loved being with a crowd of journalists because they good-naturedly questioned me on my metaphysical and spiritual beliefs. None of them concluded I was crazy. They just warned me that other people would say I was. I thanked them and moved on.

I'm Not Over Exercise

I exercise now because it makes me feel more healthy. That is a good mind-set to adhere to. I hike in the hills with my dog Terry because we both love it. I just have to be careful in rain or snow so that I don't slip and take a fall.

Exercise classes are too driven by the mirror. I'm over that. I'd rather be in nature. It's more fun and I can let my mind roam with each step without an instructor screaming encouragements at me.

I observe a low-carbohydrate diet because it makes me feel better. But not too low. If I don't have enough carbs, I don't sleep well. Everyone is different. I have to have at least two slices of bread a day, usually at breakfast. I also have to have a little dark chocolate every day. Dark chocolate is good for the pancreas and milk chocolate is good for something else I can't remember, but I don't like it much anyway.

I've developed an extended tummy, which means I like trousers with a forgiving waistline. I went to a plastic surgeon and asked him if liposuction would help. He said no, at my age he couldn't get to the fat underneath. And he said I'd have to go on a starvation diet to lose the stomach accumulation. I decided to relax and enjoy the reality that my dancer's figure is gone. The important thing now is to be happy and healthy.

I gave up smoking years ago when I had serious coughing attacks. I stopped cold turkey and have not missed it. I never did drink much, but I remember I was once having dinner with my friend, the composer Cy Coleman, at Trader Vic's in New York. I had too many mai tais and passed out right at the table, my head in my plate. Cy and company went right on talking until I woke up. No one said anything about it. I was glad I could still breathe despite my nose being buried in my dinner.

I've never done drugs. They never appealed to me. I smoked pot twice while on tour and practically ate the furniture in the hotel room. I never understood the intricacies of recreational drugs. Once at a party the hostess served coke in a silver bowl. I thought it was Sweet and Low and put a silver spoonful of it in my coffee—somebody later told me it was hundreds of dollars' worth. That was the last time I was invited to her house.

My life in Hollywood was never one where I socialized much. I knew most everybody, but clubs and parties were not all that attractive to me. In between pictures I preferred to get on a Pan American Flight and fly around the world, disembarking when a country called me. When you are young enough to enjoy it, that's the best kind of exercise there is.

Never Get Over Trust

I hope I will never give up my sense of trust. I believe trusting is the reason I've been safe, despite having been caught up in revolutions and protests and human schemes of all sorts.

Trust in Hollywood was more difficult. Clifford Odets called Hollywood the "Big Knife." I suppose that's true, but I found the power of trust usually trumped that of the knife. Loyalty, even in Hollywood, is revered. I never changed agents just because there was a lull in my employment. All careers have lulls. I used the lulls to travel or have a love affair. I believe in trust and its rewards. When you genuinely trust someone, even in show business, their own self-esteem usually keeps them from betraying you. At least that's been my experience. I like to be realistic, but I'm not cynical. There's no future for me in Hollywood if I let myself become cynical.

Government is another story. There's just too much that the government never tells us. I want to know the real truth behind Pearl Harbor, 9/11, why we attacked Iraq, what really happened to Amelia Earhart, why the existence of UFOs is being covered up . . . and a thousand other things. I don't consider my questions about the government's role in all these things as being cynical; I call it obsessive curiosity. I like Albert Einstein's quote: "The important thing is not to stop questioning. Curiosity has its own reason for existing."

You could say that I trust that there are many truths we don't hear about.

I'm Trying to Get Over Anger

I can get violently angry when I see an act of injustice firsthand. I get perturbed at inefficiency and impatient at a lack of work ethic. But injustice truly infuriates me, particularly injustice and cruelty directed toward innocent human beings (like small children) and animals. In fact, at times it makes me violent. I've noticed that showing my violent fury can often put a stop to the injustice I've encountered.

I have stopped a parent screaming at and hitting a child by working myself up to the point where I almost hit the parent. It worked for a bit, but as soon as I walked away, the parent was at it again. Once when I was mugged on the street in New York, I screamed and babbled and flung my arms around like a crazy person. Crazy terrifies people! That mugger ran away as fast as he could.

I was so angry when Nixon invaded Cambodia that I threw a chair at the television set. When W Bush invaded Iraq

with his "shock and awe," I screamed at the television until
my voice was gone.

But I've never gotten really angry at anything to do with
my career or Hollywood. Several producers I know say anger
is what keeps them going, what fuels their creative impulses.
I don't feel that way. Thanks to my belief in karma, I know it
will all come out in the wash.

I have done several independent films where I never got
paid what I'd been promised. There's no point in suing. That
would just cost more. So I wait. I know karma will work its
balance. The laws of cause and effect apply in any situation
and endeavor. We are all actors on the stage of life and I am
creating my own part—even if I don't always get rewarded for
it in the ways or in the time frame I expected!

I Will Never Get Over the Thrill of Live Performing

When you are performing live, your health is everything. Your entire life is prioritized according to what is expected of you on stage that night. There can be no running for a cab in the rain, in case you slip and fall; no wine at lunch or dinner; no screaming with laughter until you're hoarse. No love affair that renders you anxious or unhappy, and no love affair that makes you want to hurry through the show and get back to making love. There is no other life when you are performing live. But the rewards are worth it. When a live audience is moved to silence in a theater, the Greeks used to say they were experiencing their Godhead. That's why it's divine. Silence is your new "God-speak," when you understand and have proof that you've captured their attention completely. But you have to be healthy or you can't do it night after night.

Performing live in front of an audience is the ultimate test of self-identity. The audience wants to know who you are above all else. They will never respond to artifice or show business trickery. They want the real you.

That means you have to be willing to tell them. You have to become one of them. You have to become ultra-aware of everything around you. You see no one out there in the dark when you are performing, and yet you are one with them. You are one with the big black giant seated in front of you, and you are a Big Happy.

The miraculous magic of self-expression and the appreciation the audience feels overrides everything. You and they are one, a conglomeration of souls, simultaneously giving and receiving. Souls creating a new reality with a subliminal awareness that we are all one. You bend and flow and soar with the music. You allow it to carry you aloft. You begin to fill every space with body language; no movement is meaningless.

The lights amplify what you are doing and you know the audience can see everything. You are completely exposed. There are levels of subtlety in the music you never realized were there. You forget all the pain you ever felt. You forget technique, anxiety, and everything you ever learned. In fact, you forget who you are, because you have become one with the audience, one with the music, the lights, and the collective spirit of the audience. They send you energy. You send it back. You participate with each other. You are dancing and moving in the light with God.

Yes, it is better than sex. It is being One with all there is.

I Am Trying to Get Over the Feeling That the World Is Falling Apart

For me these are very difficult days. I find myself overcome with sadness a lot of the time. If I see innocent animals and children hurt, I feel tears sliding down my cheeks and my chest contracts into a tightness that makes me know I'm holding back an avalanche of despair.

The news on TV and in the papers is awful. People everywhere (particularly the young) are rude and insensitive. Computerized voices replace real people at the end of every phone call. People email instead of talking to each other, so no emotion is exchanged. Dogs and cats wander the streets because their owners have been evicted from their homes and couldn't take them. Small shops and businesses are going out of business so the only place to shop is Walmart.

The weather is so erratic and dangerous, it is almost as though God is angry. People are fighting with each other all over the world. It costs one million dollars per soldier per year for our "protective exploits" overseas, while people are living on bread and water here at home—and even the water isn't clean. Our skies are polluted. Out-of-control traffic turns streets into parking lots. Crime is reported like the stock market or sports scores.

Great and proud producers of pictures in days gone by have been foreclosed upon and are now living with their children. Hollywood is slow to dead, except for disaster films, tent pole pictures, and those featuring young, sexy vampires.

People greet each other saying they are fine; no one really says what they are feeling, particularly news anchors who chirp on and on like lunatic birds, joking and teasing each other as though what they've just reported has no meaning. Gossip is the entertainment of the day, preferably of the negative sort, so that the rest of us will feel better about ourselves.

The poles are melting. Seas are rising, expectations are lowering, God's in his heaven, and all is *not* right with the world.

What do we do to feel better? We can't say it's all not real. The world is too much with us for that.

I find that if I go out into Mother Nature, I calm down. She has a rhythm that has outlasted all else—even what we do to her. I try to take on her rhythm. It's more calm and understanding. I try to melt away from the pot-boiling present by enveloping myself with the sounds and sweet movement of the trees and clouds and insects and animals around me. They know what is happening, and they are prepared to be patient and wait. It's as though all life around me understands the flow of time except for we humans.

Then, after a while, I begin to understand the Big Truths better. I can see that all life is cyclical. What is happening has happened before and will happen again. This realization makes me feel better because I know this too shall pass. We know we have to get through the night in order to have the day.

I realize we and nature are part of a much larger pattern. We understand the cycles of the seasons and the cycles of night and day. We need to understand more fully the cycles of the stars, which on a much grander scale show us the cyclical energy that makes us behave the way we do.

Suddenly the personality aspects of the zodiac don't seem so silly. The procession of the equinoxes contains the probabilities of human and natural behavior. The ancients knew this and regulated their lives in large part according to the knowledge they had of the movement of the stars. Does that mean that stars have personalities, and the movement of the stars is the expression of those personalities?

If so, then the age of Pisces (with the two fish swimming in opposite directions) would indeed exemplify the age we're living in. And Aquarius (the water bearer) would exemplify a new beginning and rebirth.

It's time. I'll carry some water.

I'm Not Over Having
My Hair Colored

I couldn't tell you what the real color of my hair is now. Somewhere between white and faded mouse gray. When I'm guerrilla traveling and away from a hair salon, it can really be embarrassing. But I don't have a mirror with me anyway. So who is it really embarrassing for? To be without a mirror for a month or so is an interesting experience. The image of your physical self you carry in your head becomes unreal.

When I worked with Jerzy Kosinski, the author of *Being There,* he told me that he needed to have his picture taken every day and he needed to look at it to prove to himself that he was still alive. His wife was a photographer, which I suppose made it easier. His brilliance as a writer was matched only by his own inner anger. His childhood and background were horrendous. He was abused and abandoned, and for years he didn't speak. This identity surfaced in the characters he wrote (Chauncey Gardiner for one). Sometimes when we spoke of his past he would plunge a knife into the top of his desk and draw it across, making a deep gash in the surface. For so many of us, self-image and anger are intertwined. Who do we believe we really are? And who will remind us if we don't remind ourselves?

Which leads me back to having my hair colored. I know that who I really am is inside of me. That's why I don't need a mirror or a photograph to see my true self. Still, as long as I can, I'll try to make the outside match the spirit I feel on the inside—and for now that means keeping my hair the color I see when I close my eyes.

Sex Got Over Me

Sex is so complicated that the only way to discuss it is *simply*.

I have had many love affairs. I have not had many sex affairs. I was not sophisticated enough for that. I had to have the emotional component. That's when it gets complicated.

I have found that since sex and I have somewhat gotten over each other in my advancing years, it is such a relief. My relationships with my male friends are less fraught and more equal and honest. We tell each other the truth when the sexual component slows down. I never think about who's gay and who's straight anymore.

My close female friends (for whom sex is also slowing down) are my friends for life. We talk about what we did for love and what it felt like when that sexual feeling slunk away. We agree it isn't anything that drives us to therapy. It is more a question of taking melatonin and estrogen and other chemicals we don't produce much anymore. None of us were ever into anything like bondage or S&M or the like. If that

had been the case, we probably could have acted out the the-
atricality of it and continued on. Instead, sex usually got pretty
funny, faking orgasms and all. I was the acting coach in the
group. Questions came up like whether it made sense to still
feel possessive of a partner when you weren't having much sex
anymore, or how to handle jealousy, and whether we should
be liberal in what our men still wanted to partake of.

When I look back over my life, I wonder what I was doing
with all my hormones and attraction and longings, when I
always so strongly felt the need for freedom. Most of the men
I was with wanted to get married. I was already married
and stayed that way precisely so it wouldn't really become an
issue. My husband and I had a liberal arrangement regarding
each other's lovers. We were friends. We stayed married so we
wouldn't be tempted to marry again. I don't understand the
need for the institution and I could never live a life where I felt
tied down to a promise just because my love hormones were
raging at the time I promised. After almost thirty years of
marriage, my husband and I divorced and he has since passed
on. I am living alone with my darling dog Terry, with my
creativity, my friends who come over, and the freedom I have
always loved and continue to cherish. Sex is not a dead issue
for me, but basically it is a *non-issue*—and, in point of fact, I
think it always was.

Because of my detachment regarding sexual behavior, I
have nothing invested in my curiosity at what other people
do. I really don't care about the particulars of somebody's sex

life, but I am extremely interested in how sex came into being in the first place. Just as I investigate life after death, and life before life, I would seriously like to know how sex came about. I would like to share with you a few past-life experiences I have had that gave me a clue.

I vividly remember being androgynous in the Lemurian (pre-Atlantis) time period. My state of being and that of others around me was peaceful and serene. Procreation occurred through the power of the mind in deep meditation. Each of us had male and female genitalia but what was important was the desire of the soul, which was made manifest through connecting to the God source. Each human had an equal vibration of yin and yang, female and male.

At some point in Lemurian history some of us became intrigued with the idea of dividing the yin and the yang vibration so we could observe the other with more objectivity. I was one of those who agreed to participate in what came to be called sexual division. Today every culture on Earth has a myth that describes the equivalent of Eve being born out of the rib of Adam. Out of one came two. That is what I remember experiencing. I remember the ceremony and the attendant spiritual practitioners and masters. I was immersed in a tank of very thick water which was also infused with light. Each of my seven chakra centers was open and receptive. I felt peaceful and willing to be divided. The spiritual practitioner meditated on a ray of light coming from above, which included all the seven colors of the rainbow—one for each chakra. I joined the meditation of the spiritual practitioners as the light went down the center of my physical body, separating each chakra in half. We knew in those days that the physical body was what we had created from coagulated thought. We knew we had created our bodies with our celestial thought patterns.

Slowly, my body began to separate into two vibrations—one yin and one yang. Each was equal to the other. I directed my soul to enter the female side of my separated body. On cue, my soul mate, who was present, entered the male side. The sexual division was complete. Out of the androgynous body two were born: one male, one female—each with an inculcated soul. From then on I felt as a human being that I would always look for my other half.

What transpired next was fascinating. My other half and I had a sexual consciousness of zero. The idea of sex had never occurred to us before because we each had lived in an androgynous equal vibration. As we viewed each other separately, we were overwhelmed by the beauty of the colors of the chakra system in our other half. The colors of the chakras became the attraction if we then decided to procreate. The power of the color vibration (every color has a vibration) drew us together until our bodies touched and the separate male and female genitalia came together.

I remember this very well, and when I did guided meditations in my Higher Self Seminars in the 80s, I included this past life experience of mine. Many people told me they felt comfortable with this idea that eons ago they had agreed to sexual division, too. Since we now know that all time is occurring at once, my students allowed themselves to go back because it was happening *now*.

The laws of vibrational attraction are still in play today. We don't know why we are so attracted to someone, but there it is. I think so many people are looking for their soul mate because they know it's the other half of their previously androgynous self. The male became the outward, aggressive expressor, the female the more hidden understander of the innate spiritual connection to God. The melding together of the yin and yang vibration is what sex is.

One of the explanations for homosexuality and transgenderism could, I believe, be a profound identification with a recent incarnation as a member of the opposite sex. I believe each one of us has had both male and female lifetimes. As we make our soul's journey through time, I think resistance to reincarnational understanding is because we feel threatened by our sexual identity. We just don't like to contemplate seriously that we might have been a member of the opposite sex in a previous incarnation. Questions of sex and spiritual understanding of the soul are intertwined.

What each soul experiences through the march of time only adds to the complications of what sex has become nowadays. Who knows what the soul journey of a rapist or a pedophile or a suicide bomber or any other distorted soul's experience might have been. I don't excuse any of that behavior, but I believe such people are negative teachers for us to study and learn from. An eye for an eye is not a punitive belief for me, but rather a karmic belief. What one commits, one receives. Though perhaps not in the time period we judge is fair.

Perhaps Hollywood is the purveyor of so much sexual violence these days because it is high time we learn more of who we are and have been. If we learned more about the soul's journey through time in our educational system, we'd have a more peaceful and less violent world regardless of what God we believe in.

Another fascinating story of the birth of human sexuality can be traced to a set of Sumerian cuneiform tablets. These tablets are ancient, created long before Egypt became a great civilization, and have been translated by Zacharia Sitchin, Paul Van Ward, William Bramley, and others. They tell quite a story: a story of visitations by the Annunaki people who came to Earth from a planet called Nibiru. It is apparently a planet much larger than Earth and is called the Planet of the Crossing because it crosses our solar system in regular, cyclical time periods. The tablets say the Annunaki seeded the human race by genetically engineering their own DNA.

The tablets tell the story of much sexual perversion, unrest, and predatory behavior. Perhaps we have a bit of Annunaki DNA in our strands and have inherited some behavior patterns from our original parents. The cosmos is so immense and, I believe, teeming with all kinds of life that we probably were seeded by many cosmic visitors who see us as their protégés. Some abductees have reported hearing their abductors say, "Our forefathers were your forefathers." Even cosmic visitors seem to have a problem with saying *foremothers*. There could be no sex without both. I am one of the sexual foremothers of the future where hopefully sex and its theater of expression will be more balanced.

I'm Over Being Polite to People with Closed Minds

I must do my best to get over feeling frustrated and impatient with people who are wedded to *not* thinking.

I don't know why they do it. Or maybe they don't *do* anything. Maybe they just *are* in the point of view they won't give up. And each point of view has been schooled and developed by religion, social mores, and parental influence. Okay, we know all that. Maybe the operative block is fear of the unknown. Fear is taught. Babies are usually born without fear. They have to learn it. And the teachers are expert. Oscar Hammerstein was insightful when he wrote the lyrics to "You've Got to Be Taught" for *South Pacific*: *Carefully taught to fear and hate all the things your relatives hate.* As I see it, the question is: are these blocks inherent in our DNA? Can we trace them back to our origins?

For me, it's not enough simply to say that God created mankind. Many translations of ancient religious texts, including the Torah and the Mahabharata, say Eloheim created all. But the word "Eloheim" is plural. So who were these Gods? And did these Gods carry a sort of DNA karma within their soul memory? If so, then I believe every living sentient being carries some form of karma within.

So each time I'm with someone who is shockingly closed-minded, I will try to remember they have a soul history I don't know or understand. I guess that is the meaning of compassion and tolerance. Perhaps the fear of thinking openly is passed down in our DNA. And fear promulgates aggression and ultimately Evil. So is turning the other cheek the solution because it neutralizes the karma of a negative action? Even in the face of hostile, warlike aggression, the key is to understand no one loses his life. He just incurs more karmic experience. He might lose or cause someone else to lose this incarnation but not his life. Life is eternal. So why have war at all? It's ridiculous.

Many fundamentalists are just not open-minded enough to think for themselves. Neither are most traditional scientists. They always need hard physical evidence to believe something is true and real. How would they react if it were proved that physical reality itself is an illusion?

I must remember that closed-mindedness is nothing more than the loss of memory of who we really are.

I'm Over
Conservatives and Liberals

How does a person know whether they are liberal or conservative? When do these values assert themselves, and when do they start?

My mother was a Canadian with a decidedly royalist reflex. By that I mean that she revered the British royal family to such an extent that my father was often moved to make fun of her for her devotion. She always bristled, and on it went. Mother was a very loving and sensitive person, but I would have to say that about most things she was conservative. I don't think she ever thought that much about a label for herself. Her father (my grandfather, whom I never knew) was an accomplished brain surgeon in Canada and a 33rd Degree Mason. Mother never told me about his Masonic ties; I learned about them by reading his obituary in some old Canadian newspaper clippings she had saved. To be a 33rd Degree Mason is no small accomplishment. Simply put, he was well versed in metaphysics and in keeping secrets. Mother certainly inherited his gift for the latter, and because she was an accomplished gardener, she could also grasp my growing belief in reincarnation. She said she could understand living many lives because that's what her rose bushes did. Same plant, different roses every year.

Whenever I brought my books home to read to them, neither she nor Daddy had any problems with my expanding belief system. She was a student of the patterns of nature; he'd had an out-of-body experience after a near fatal car crash, as well as a visitation from his best buddy who died on the battlefield during World War II. When Daddy told me about the night he cracked up his car, he described a terrible crash and said he had essentially died. He went through a tunnel (a familiar description in many out-of-body experiences) and encountered his own mother and father, plus friends on the other side. He said he knew he was going toward God and it would be like going home to him. However, he said, a guide of some sort stopped him from going all the way to the end of the tunnel (dying) and said he needed to go back because he had more work to do. The guide told my father that his son (my brother) needed him as well as his wife (Mother), but that I really didn't. Dad said he obeyed the guide, came back into his body, and felt the pain of his injuries and found himself inside the wrecked car.

The moment that he had a vision of his war buddy on the battlefield was important to him because it made him realize that the soul must live on after death. When he checked on the time of his friend's death, he found it was exactly the same time as Daddy had seen him.

These two incidents stayed with him for his whole life, and he understood my fascination with such things completely. When we had discussions about the afterlife, he said he absolutely believed in its existence because his own near-death experience was too beautiful to deny. What he couldn't understand was *why* anyone would want to come back to live another life.

So my parents were very open-minded to all manner of esoteric subjects due to their own personal beliefs and experiences. When it came to politics, it was another story.

First of all, Mother had a sister who was married to a communist and was also the editor of the *Daily Worker* in Toronto, Canada. When Mother decided (at Daddy's urging) to become an American citizen, I remember Daddy taking the whole family through Washington, D.C., many times, declaiming about the grandeur of its architecture and the meaning of democracy. To Mother, it felt as if he were rubbing her nose in our nation's revolutionary history and break with England. He was proud of America's decision to break away from the British royal hierarchy and class-bound social structure. Perhaps Daddy was also attempting to dissuade Mother of any communist leanings just in case she, like her sister, harbored any such notions.

I remember Daddy didn't trust Henry Wallace because he was a socialist, and he thought Roosevelt was being too liberal in even *talking* to Joseph Stalin. Since Dad was from a small Virginia town named Front Royal (ironic name for his hometown!), he was a Mason-Dixon Line southerner who still called black people niggers and saw nothing demeaning in it.

I was brought up by Dora, our black nanny, and Daddy could always tell (as if by telepathy) whether she was going to be sick or pregnant! He was never wrong. I don't know what their intuitive connection was, but it was deep. I played with Dora's kids all the time. I don't remember Daddy ever having a problem with that, or his being anything but polite and kind to Dora and her family.

We were middle-class people, living a middle-class life in a neighborhood with a slight variation of architecture in each house. (Very slight.) We lived a "don't rock the boat" emotional life, which I believe ultimately made me into an eccentric because I felt I had to rebel. I attended school and dancing class every day of my life and babysat for extra money. I didn't learn much in school (except how to be a fast typist), but I did devote myself to becoming popular. Hence my football captain boyfriend and my time served as a cheerleader. I was a straight A student (so why didn't I learn anything?) and was a member of a sorority called the Sub Deb Club.

My favorite subject was geometry. (I felt I somehow knew about pyramids and the inherent brilliance of the mathematics of shapes and forms.) I rode in cars with boys, smoked only where I wouldn't get caught, and stayed a virgin even though the petting got hot and heavy. My favorite book was called

Heroes of Civilization (I still have it on my bookshelf), and
my favorite piece of music was the "Pas de Deux" from *The
Nutcracker Suite.*

I was not particularly religious, even though it said Baptist
on my birth certificate, and until I read *Cosmic Memory* by
Rudolf Steiner, I hadn't contemplated such things as reincarnation and soul searching, but I always did love to think and
discuss. At our Sunday dinners, which consisted of meatloaf,
scalloped potatoes, scalloped tomatoes, and chocolate cake
with hot chocolate sauce, Daddy used to ask me deep questions. I loved lingering over the food and discussing philosophy. Once I asked him why everything one did had so much
trouble attached to it. I was twelve. He was delighted because
he had written a doctorate of philosophy and psychology
at Johns Hopkins. He and my mother were teachers, even
though I think they loved drama more (they were like vaude-
villians together). Daddy and I talked philosophy for hours.
He was comfortable with abstract thinking and stimulated
me to come up with my own conclusions.

He was a contradiction. He was a bigoted southerner, yet
sobbed in admiration at *Raisin in the Sun.* He loved Sidney
Poitier and Sammy Davis Jr., but wouldn't let me bring either
home because of what the neighbors might say. Black people
weren't the only ones. I had a Jewish boyfriend of whom he
inquired once, "Where are your horns?"

He cried at "The Star Spangled Banner" and fervently
believed in the freedom of political dissent. He didn't like the

communists because "They'll take all our money and take us over too." One of his most advanced accomplishments at Johns Hopkins was a paper proving that color and music had a vibrational frequency that was healing, and that these vibrations corresponded equally to vibrations in the human body. I later learned he was talking about the color and energy centers of the body the ancient Hindus called *chakras,* but he didn't know that. He never finished his paper. In fact, he didn't finish much of anything. He was a brilliant and loving man, but he had no "stick-to-it-ivity." Hence I became an overachiever. He used to call me "a do-gooder," always for the underdog. Maybe to me *he* was the underdog and I wanted to do good for him.

Everything we do and are starts with family and ends with family.

I Am Over
Getting Over Family

What gives each of us more grief, and more love, than family? But grief and love produce guilt. So family = guilt.

If someone tells me they had a happy childhood, I tell them they haven't really looked at it. I believe we choose the mother, father, sisters, and brothers according to what we need to learn for our own soul's growth.

I have learned that each of us belongs to a "soul group"—that is, a conglomeration of souls we know who have known us over eons of time. So each member of that group can be a brother or sister, mother or father, and so on. Each member of the group has varied and intimate knowledge of every other member. Therefore, when an incarnation takes place and we make a choice on a cosmic higher level to be part of a family, each member starts out knowing what he or she is doing within the family. But as we grow from birth we forget why we chose to be members of that family, and because the family lessons are the most difficult of all in life, we play a blame game or we don't get the lessons at all, kidding ourselves into believing everything is happy and perfect.

Life on Earth is not meant to be easy. It is meant to be a learning experience. Of course in the final analysis our soul's goal is peace and happiness, but to get there can be difficult. Each member of the family, *on a soul level,* understands the baggage of karma each other member has. In other words, a cruel mother is understood on some level to have been treated cruelly at some time on her soul's journey. A victim has probably victimized another. These past karmic dramas need not always have occurred within the present family. It's the experience that matters, not the individual driving it.

The family is the preparation for life. But after the preparation (at age 21 or so), we are on our own. When we look back and blame a family member, it's a waste of energy and time. We should get over it.

Of course, psychotherapy helps, but I would recommend some past life therapy so we can pinpoint *why* such dramas occurred. I have been through many past life sessions where members of my family were involved. They were remarkable. I knew I wasn't making it up because of the emotion involved. I cried, laughed, screamed, and finally nodded with understanding in my soul as to why certain people and events occurred like they did.

Past life regression sessions come in very handy while going through a divorce too. And it saves each party anguish *and* money when they understand the past life karma of it all. There's no point in my going into detail regarding who did what to whom in my own life. The understanding of the karmic emotion of it all is what is important. The laws of cause and effect are in play all the time, in every moment of our lives. I wish that this law was part of our education. As my father said once, "It's too bad we have to get close to dying before we understand what it was all about in the first place."

As he lay dying, he would visit his mother and father in his sleep every night. The doctors and nurses at Johns Hopkins Hospital crowded around his bed every morning to hear what he told them. They had heard it from many dying patients before. My dad was not on medication that would have produced delusions. The dying process was the "knowing the truth" process.

My mother, on the other hand, in her last days didn't visit her relatives as greeters to heaven. She went back in time to when she was a very young girl. She talked to her mother and sisters in the past, working out problems that had occurred. She also was living what had been her dreams and fantasies when she was young. She created the reality of living what she had dreamed of. It was fascinating for me to hear and observe. I was on location with *Guarding Tess* when she passed away. We were shooting in Baltimore, where she had met and married my father and had conceived me. I believe she chose to cross over while I was there because she knew it was familiar territory to both of us.

I got a call from her nurse telling me she had taken her last breath, but I already knew it because a few minutes before the call, the alarm spontaneously went off in the house I was renting. Mother's voice came into my head and told me exactly where to locate the alarm in the house. I went straight to it (on a high shelf in a hall closet) and turned it off. Mother then instructed me to drive to my childhood home in Arlington, Virginia. I called the set, explained what had happened and told them I wouldn't be able to come in that day. They said, "Go, no problem."

I drove to the house in Virginia. In my head, mother's voice instructed me to go to a drawer that I hadn't known existed in a cupboard. Inside the drawer, I found an envelope. I opened it and read the letter inside. It was about some unflattering things involving my ex-husband. She then said she hadn't wanted to tell me because I needed to learn it all for myself.

Then she directed me to my father's underwear drawer in his bedroom. She said there would be a valentine under the clothes. There was. She instructed me to keep it. She directed me to another desk where she kept some poems. I never knew the location of any of these things. I found the poems and keep them to this day.

When I returned to Baltimore and the house I was renting, I opened the front door and the lights flicked on and off by themselves. Then the TV in the living room went on and off. I knew it was Mother saying she was with me. She then said, "Look out at the swans on the lake. I will be with them, watching you till you finish your picture."

As I looked out the window, a pair of swans glided into view on the lake.

I never broke down over either of my parents' passing, because I knew that was just what had happened—they had passed. They didn't die. Their souls are with me when I need some advice or have a good laugh at the absurdity of what we believe is the "truth" here on Earth.

Once on my trek across Spain doing the Santiago de Compostela pilgrimage, I got lost. I ended up in some military installation, which was a real breach of security. Mom and Dad came into my head and showed me the path back to the Camino. Then I could feel each of them say goodbye to each other and go back to their own school of learning where they were.

Family is important because they are our first teachers. We are known to each other. That is why it is so hard to grow away from them. Twins always recognize each other for life. Mothers sometimes remember they were fathers before, and vice versa. The family tree of relatives, of aunts and uncles, etc., is made up of members of the soul group we each belong to.

When this spiritual knowledge is applied to the problems we have with our families, the psychodramas that we are all a part of become easier to bear and certainly educational. Forgive and forget becomes possible because we remember.

It's good to clear up the problems with family because, if not, we'll go around again at a future date.

I Am Over Going to Funerals

I never liked funerals. I remember the funeral of a despised Hollywood mogul. So many people attended that someone quipped, "Gee, give the people what they want and they really will show up!"

I like paying respects to a life well lived, but I know the person we are mourning is not dead. And the idea of getting closure? Why say that? The departed one has just gone on to another level of understanding.

When someone I love passes on, I go immediately to a place where I spent time with them. I sit there and call them to me, just to know they're still around. Usually, I can feel them and they feel better that I don't feel sad. I feel people don't want to "die" because they know that those left behind will feel sad and bereft. Maybe more of us would go sooner if we knew it would be all right with those who are left behind.

I appreciate what Dr. Kevorkian does because he respects the desires of those who want to move on and are not afraid to die. But I have one caveat to my agreement with him. Spiritually speaking, I wonder if a life is meant to be lived out to its complete finish because of the soul lessons to be learned, not only by the person passing on, but also those close to him or her. Dying is as important as birth. The way we die is as important as anything we will ever do.

I personally remember having committed a cosmic suicide by cutting the silver cord attaching my soul to my body. I did it because I couldn't bear to see what was happening to the Atlantean civilization around me. It was crumbling, sinking, and full of sorrow. I remember soaring above what was occurring in an out-of-body experience and deciding to cut the silver cord. I feel that that was a cowardly decision when I meditate on it now. I should have experienced what everyone else was going through.

I get very depressed over the way things are going in the world today. If I feel I am experiencing too painful a transition when my time comes, I will make my decision then as to what I will do . . . how I will go. Maybe I'll even get some help from those I know I will meet on the other side.

I Can't Remember if I'm Over Memory Loss

I have given up being concerned about my short-term memory loss. I never remember where I put my car keys, and then when I finally find them I can't remember what they're for!

I have decided that what I can't remember is still in there somewhere and can be retrieved in time if I give up trying. Perhaps what I can't remember is not all that important anyway. What's in a name? What's in the memory of an event that didn't mean all that much? Perhaps memory loss happens in order that we live more in the Now.

I have come to be more relaxed with my memory loss because I feel I've gained more of the totality of Now. I wouldn't like to have amnesia, but perhaps my brain doesn't want to be filled with facts and figures that have nothing to do with what lies ahead.

I'm learning more to let go and let God, as they say. I do write down schedules and appointments and I'm training myself to always put my car keys in the same place. Anyway, the secret to happiness is good health and a bad memory.

Never Get Over a Dog—
Get Another One

I have never known friendship
and companionship like Terry. I know I've known her before,
in Egypt, I think, when she was an Annubis, a God of the
Netherworld. She looks just like an Annubis.

Perhaps I am bonded so closely to her because we are together every moment of the day and night. We travel in cars
and airplanes together; she has her own seat. When I'm working, she is in my trailer waiting for me in between set-ups. She
knows me better than any other living being and vice versa.
She knows what I am thinking at all times and vice versa.

Sometimes she will sit by the door wanting to go out in a
room far away, and I feel it. Her want is my command. She
knows it, too. But she never abuses her power over me. We
sleep cuddled up together every night. It's a good thing that I
don't have a man in my life.

The spiritual bond is awe-inspiring. She's beginning to get
white whiskers now, and she is eleven years old. Already I'm

rearranging where we will sleep in the house so she won't have to negotiate the stairs. I want to get another brother or sister for her so I will have a reminder when she finally decides to go. But she won't let me. All I have to do is think about another dog and she won't speak to me.

Last Halloween I was speaking to the woman who runs the animal shelter here in Santa Fe. I wanted to come by and look at a possible little Chihuahua for Terry. I could feel Terry listening to the conversation. We were in a store in the mall. Children and trick-and-treaters, ghosts and goblins, popping sounds, candy and chaos abounded as I was talking to my friend about a sister or brother for Terry. I looked away, then back again to Terry. She had jumped from her chair where she always sits and disappeared. I dropped everything and waded into the sea of Halloween trick-or-treaters. Terry was gone—nowhere to be seen. The word went out that "Shirley's Terry has run away."

Someone called the shop I was in. "She was here," they said, "but we put her outside." I was a frantic person. Would someone in the crowd step on her? Would she get hit by a car? I ran around like a crazy woman for fifteen minutes, trying to calm myself by remembering that she had a chip and a phone number on her collar. Then the woman from the animal shelter called for me over the crowd. She was holding Terry in her arms. It was as though Terry told her to tell me she didn't want anyone else, and why didn't I understand that.

She knew exactly what she had done. Now I knew what I should do—nothing!

So, for now we have each other, for another few years, I am sure.

I've often wondered how I would put up with her possessiveness if she were a man. But that's the point. I'd rather have a good, funny, loyal dog than a man. It's taken me a few senior years to come to that conclusion and I'm happier for it. The depth of our connection and love is unmatched. We take turns as to who is in charge; she is easy to cook for; she doesn't drink, smoke, or do drugs; and she doesn't suffer from any kind of macho deficiencies.

We like the same sleeping conditions (cool with the window open) and enjoy the same movies before sleep, although being a rat terrier, her favorite film is *Stuart Little*. She's seen it many times. We like to watch nature documentaries where the animals run around happily, and she gets her indoor exercise jumping up to the television set. We take a long hike together every day. We have a bear who watches us sometimes, but Terry knows it and maintains her 26-pound superiority to such an extent that the bear just leaves us alone.

Terry knows when there is someone coming or at the door long before I do and is much happier to see them than I am. I fight against being a recluse, but she makes it extremely attractive.

She is the love of my life and any other in the near future.

We have an agreement that she will come back immediately after she leaves. I trust that and my love for her brings me to tears because she has made me know, understand, and love myself more. She has made it possible for me to know that I am capable of unconditional love. I never knew that before.

That's what dogs are for: unconditional love. They live on a level of spirit that we humans would like to achieve. They are without guile and are clever in how they show us the truth. They know we are a little backward in our understanding of what's really important and will be patient with our slow learning and our impatient and dictatorial orders up to a point. But when a dog sits down and refuses to budge, we know we should look at ourselves. It's that simple.

The secrets of the universe are in a dog's eyes. Their eyes convey the patient wisdom of a collective understanding. That's why everybody should have one.

I Wonder If I Will Be
Over the Drama of 2012

I have spent a great deal of time and energy studying what has been written about 2012 by the experts who have dedicated their lives to the mysteries of the Mayan calendar and the scientists who have made life studies of the movements of the planets in time. As the 2012 date approaches, there will be much speculation as to whether the world will come to an end or another Y2K fizzle will occur.

This is what I've learned.

For the first time in 26,000 years our solar system will be in direct alignment with the center of our galaxy. The distance between our planet and center of the galaxy will be approximately 26,000 light years. The average life span of the human is 26,000 days. From the perspective of sacred and celestial science, these facts are shadows of a more galactic harmony. These are not presumptions of the Mayan calendar. These are facts supported by those who study the heavens.

On December 21, 2012, the precession of the equinoxes will end and a new precession will begin. The great cycle began in August 3014 BCE, the approximate time of the first Egyptian hieroglyphics. The great cycle will end on December 21, 2012, when our sun will move into direct alignment with the equator of the Milky Way galaxy. Science acknowledges that this galactic alignment will occur and that the Mayan calendar marks the event.

The question is: What will it mean? Will it mean a polar shift as some have predicted and have written—that the sun will rise in the south and set in the north? Some computers predict that a magnetic pole reversal could bring about the end of civilization, and worse, that the Earth would be left with no magnetic field at all. We don't know what happened 26,000 years ago when this alignment last happened.

The Mayan people and their culture came suddenly and left suddenly, after three hundred years. Some call them the surfers of the universe. When they left their calendar, what were they trying to tell us?

Magnetic reversals have happened, according to science, 171 times in the last 76 million years, with at least 14 of the reversals occurring in the last 4.5 million years alone. Some mainstream scientists suggest we are overdue for a polar shift. Some say we are in the early stages of just such a reversal, which explains our erratic weather patterns, the short circuitry of our consciousness, and the weakening of the planet's magnetic field.

In July 2004 *The New York Times* dedicated its Science section to describing what a magnetic reversal is. "The collapse of the Earth's magnetic field, which both guards the planet and guides many of its creatures, appears to have started in earnest about 150 years ago." Many scientists believe this is true. They feel that the more it weakens, the *faster* it weakens. Thus an abrupt climate change accompanies the weakening. We recall the woolly mammoths believed to have been caught in a polar reversal during the last ice age, frozen in midstride with their latest meals still in their mouths—proof that climate change happens very fast with pole reversal when the magnetic field weakens.

We know the sun is going through a magnetic shift now. ✳ The Earth appears to be in the early stages of a polar reversal. So what does this mean?

Our brains detect magnetic changes because our brains contain millions of tiny magnetic particles. These particles connect us to the Earth's magnetic field in a powerful and intimate way which affects our consciousness profoundly. Our nervous systems are affected, our immune systems, and even our perceptions of reality. Our dreams, our thoughts, our emotions, and our understanding of time and space are thrown out of balance when the magnetic field is weaker.

We could say, though, that out of balance could also mean an expanded reality. The Earth's magnetics play an important role in how our consciousness functions. It is happening to me every day, every hour. I move from one room to another to tend to something and I find that I've already done it. In other words, my perceptions of time are askew. I'm living in the past and the future simultaneously.

Many of my friends tell me the same thing. It's not just short-term memory confusion. It's bigger than that. It's a new perception of reality.

If the magnetic fields on Earth are a kind of magnetic glue which designates our reality, when that glue shifts it throws off our perception of what is real. At first I thought it was just ageing. But some of my young friends in their twenties and thirties are experiencing the same thing.

Using magnetic glue as the visual model, it seems that the stronger the magnetic glue, the more our consciousness is tied to traditional behavior, old mores and existing beliefs. In places where the magnetic glue is weaker, the more our consciousness longs for change.

We know there are places in the world where the magnetic fields are stronger and weaker. They can be measured. For example, the places on our planet that have the lowest magnetic intensity are under the Suez Canal and into Israel. Hence, change is occurring every day in an attempt to evolve to new understandings. In other parts of the Middle East there are conflicting magnetic fields, which also reflect the struggle between old, traditional ways and the compulsion for change.

Another low magnetic field runs parallel to the west coast of America. Hence, change happens in human consciousness more swiftly. Stretching from Southern California to northern

Washington is a low magnetic field, thus innovative ideas in science, technology, fashion, music, art, and films occur. In central Russia are some of the strongest magnetic fields. The people there tend to cling to tradition and change comes slowly.

Even without "scientific" evidence, we know intuitively that we are affected by the magnetic forces of the planets: astrology, the full moon, etc. I know artists who can be creative only with a full moon.

Our consciousnesses directly affect whatever happens in our world. The retarded consciousness of one powerful leader can take the world into war. Our beliefs affect our consciousness and our consciousness affects our reality. So we change our reality simply by how we observe it. "The greater amount of observing, the greater amount of influence." So "how" we observe creates the reality of the future.

In this way quantum physics and 2012 come together. What we *believe* will happen will be the reality, accompanied by the magnetic influence of the alignment itself. And, if we want to see our reality changed positively, we have to change how we see ourselves positively.

For me, the 2012 end date represents a cosmic choice we each must make. The power for positive change will be there, but also the power will be so strong that if we don't see ourselves and our future positively we will be bypassed. I don't believe it is the end of the world even for those who will choose to remain negative, materialistic, and cynical.

They will simply become irrelevant. For those who see a new beginning, it will be a cosmic charge of light coming from the alignment itself. Of course our new reality will be an adjustment because it *won't* include war, depletion of resources, genocide, technological abuse, anger, guilt, or hatred. In fact our adjustment will be that we won't have anything to be against! What a concept! What a cosmic shift! We will then dwell more in the inner reality of our identity which I believe we will find *enlightening,* and as a result our outer reality will shift.

So are we headed toward a catastrophe that has indeed occurred in the ancient past, or are we going to create a New Jerusalem with the magnetics of the 2012 alignment? Whatever occurred in the past didn't include the presence of 6½ billion people. At least not so far as I have read. So I wonder if the positive energy of 6½ billion people wouldn't raise the electromagnetic energy of the entire planet for thousands of years of peace.

Was that why the Mayans left the calendar that ends on December 21, 2012?

When I traveled to Mayan country (Yucatán peninsula, Guatemala, Honduras, and Belize), I asked the present-day Mayans about their ancestors. They said they came suddenly with an advanced technology and left suddenly, abandoning their greatest cities during the ninth century AD. The most valuable and sophisticated object they left behind was a calendar which calculated cosmic cycles and time. The calendar tracked galactic time and movements of the stars. In addition to that, the calendar tracks the celestial alignment of the Earth's solar system, our sun, and our Earth in relation to the center of our galaxy—an event that will not happen again for another 26,000 years.

I found these facts to be disturbing, intriguing, and certainly worthy of taking seriously where human behavior and consciousness are concerned. When I questioned the Mayan descendants about their ancestors, they said things like, "Our ancestors were timekeepers who one day left their temples and pyramids and walked into the jungle and vanished, returning to the place where they came from." They told me, "They knew something important in their time which we are just beginning to learn in ours." They didn't know what "the end of time" meant; that was the part of the ancestors' wisdom that wasn't left. Whenever I asked whether the Mayan wisdom was based on the need for us to know our true selves better, they didn't know what I was talking about. They only knew that everything was moving too fast for them.

In my conversations with Stephen Hawking, he said that the speed with which our computers are performing will soon surpass the capacity of the human brain. The computers will become ultra-intelligent thinking machines capable of much more than our brains are capable of. He questioned whether humans would then be obsolete and machines would then be the vanguard of evolution. Would humanity then have reached the end of its evolutionary journey?

I loved my talks with Hawking. We met because at one point we had the same editor in our literary lives. When he came to America I hosted a few parties for him. And when I visited him at Cambridge outside of London, he told me he could quite possibly be the reincarnation of Isaac Newton. He was born on the same date that Newton died, a hundred years later or so and, of course, he holds the Isaac Newton Chair at Cambridge. On the walls of his office at Cambridge, side by side, hung pictures of Albert Einstein and Marilyn Monroe. "Each," he said, "had beautiful curves pertaining to the universe."

It was moving for me to watch him fall in love with his nurse, divorce his wife Jane, and go through the soap opera of his life while he was confined to his wheelchair and could barely move at all. He moved around the streets of Cambridge in his wheelchair at speeds more akin to the Indianapolis 500 and laughed all the way.

We talked about the difference between information and intelligence. At the rate of speed of the information age, the growth rate of human knowledge will be reaching its own maximum. But knowledge is not the goal—wisdom is. Wisdom determines how the knowledge is used.

I'm glad to see his *Into the Universe with Stephen Hawking* is questioning extraterrestrial presence. He says his mathematical brain says there must be extraterrestrial intelligence out there. He just hopes they come in peace. *And* he speculates they might already be here.

Hawking didn't say we are a half-awake species. I am saying it. We go about our lives, our work, our shopping, our raising of children, in half-trance. We don't know what to do about the speed of life and information that we can't keep up with. We don't even know we can't keep up. We just feel it. More and more of us are asking "Who am I?" "Why am I here?" "What did I come for?" "What can I do about anything?" We derive our identity by the knowledge of our name, our job, our social security number, our address, our gender, our political and religious beliefs, our education, and our social status. But who are we really?

We are half-awake as to who we are, who we aren't, and even what our needs would be if they could be fulfilled.

I believe what we are facing in the world is a crisis of an enlightened identity. What are the roots of our human greed, our fear, our need to control weather, our capacity for abuse, our desecration of the planet and ourselves? We have sophisticated information-gathering skills and no notion how to use those skills for our happiness.

This is why people like me write books about the questionings of our true selves, where we might have come from, if we are alone in the universe, and if we are living out the laws of cause and effect. What were the ancient civilizations that we might have lived among? Did we destroy ourselves then as we seem to be doing now? How can anyone who is awake not ask these questions? That is why we don't have a sense of "I"-ness. The more "I"-ness we touch, the deeper is our sense of ease.

Yes, I have enough money, which is, unfortunately, a requirement for "ease" these days. But such a state of ease has led me to deeper questions about our addiction to materialism and more money than we need. I remember John Paul Getty's remark when he was asked if he had made enough money. He said, "Not yet." He was the richest man in the world at the time, with a face that looked poverty-stricken.

Why do we look for outside and external stimulation and acquisitions to make ourselves happy? A new car, a new dress, jewelry, etc. I feel it's because we don't feel we have enough on the inside. I remember a strange state of mind I got into while walking the Santiago de Compostela pilgrimage. I was hurting all over from bleeding blisters, the cruel sun, the aches and pains of walking twenty miles a day. I tried to find the enlightened fulfillment inside, but I found that if I concentrated on the purse I wanted to buy at a very expensive store when I returned to Madrid, I felt better. I counted the inside pockets of the purse, I felt the soft leather, I imagined where I'd wear it. I was in that state for a few hours until I realized I was trying to find comfort in the external outside world while my trust and faith in my internal self went unexamined. From then on, I asked for help from my own internal higher self. The walk became easier and I found I was connecting to some past lives I had experienced in that part of the world, which I think was one of the reasons I decided to make the pilgrimage in the first place.

We are now what we have been before, as well as what

we will be. I began to understand more fully the emotional addiction I, and others, have for "things." Simply put, material things are a replacement for the true self we haven't yet touched within ourselves. The Buddhists speak of non-attachment, which is different than detachment. I was beginning to see the difference. Our attachment to so many things makes us forget why we are here and what we are supposed to be learning about ourselves.

We are in a state of separation between spirit and matter, between our very souls and materialism. We are half-awake with our toys and technology. We don't hear our souls crying to be recognized as part of creation so we will wake up. The world we have made and live in does not bear witness to the divine. It bears witness to our greed, our delusions of power, and to the righteousness of religion. We kill for the determination of our own religious power. We kill for the individual's democratic right to plunder the Earth as we separate ourselves more and more from the Earth's divinity. We live separate from our true selves.

Will the cosmic alignment of 2012 force us magnetically to realign with why we are here? Will its effect on our consciousness bring about the enlightenment we don't even realize is missing? Perhaps galactic nature itself will force us to wake up or die of the separation from ourselves.

The ancients promised that the Earth as a living being would wake us to sing. Perhaps the alignment is how it will happen.

I Am Not Over
Good Vibrations

The Mayan science is based on frequencies of vibrationary resonance. Our science is based on matter. Our scientists say that matter is the only provable reality. With the advances in our modern science though, our scientists are coming around to understanding what the Mayans meant when they claimed that all reality is constructed of different levels of vibrational frequency. Up to now, scientists have claimed reality could be detected by our senses. They are now bowing to the possibility that there may be other realities that we cannot discern through our senses, that there may be coexisting parallel realities going on.

We, as human beings, are in resonance with our planet, as are the trees, nature, and animals. When these resonances are disturbed, so are we. We know our planet is a living, evolving organism. If we have created an imbalance through our depletion of natural resources and toxic pollution into our environment, then we must wake up to what that actually means. The 2012 alignment should take place with an Earth in balance, not an Earth out of balance.

I believe that there are other beings of intelligence in the universe, waiting and observing how we will handle this 2012 alignment. These beings are of a more advanced vibrational frequency and are waiting to be acknowledged by humans so that they can help us wake up before it is too late. They are hoping for what they call a "galactic synchronization." They know that 2012 is a major evolutionary shift. If we acknowledge them and work with them, we would all become part of a galactic civilization. The age of Universal Being Kind will begin.

I do not believe there are "evil" aliens. Producers make a lot of money on screen and in television through such an idea though, because fear makes money. The "good" alien would challenge us to be better ourselves, and we are not up to that kind of challenge right now. We are obsessed with evil, fear, protection, and the entitlement of being looked after. Abdicating self-responsibility is our middle name. We want the government, the church, and our "system" to take care of us. We don't have 50 states here in America, we have 51—the latest being the state of Denial.

I am over being taken care of. I am going to take care of myself by asking questions and studying anything I can that is innovative and makes sense to me in this new world of alignment. According to some scientists, our brains have an unbounded talent for creativity, promising that we can become whatever we imagine. Each brain is already capable of a greater number of associations than the number of atoms in the universe! And there is strong evidence that the holographic (nonlinear) universe acts as an interconnected mind to which each human being has direct access. More and more people are developing their clairvoyance, telepathy, and remote viewing. The reality of humanity's interconnected thought field is astonishing.

Some of the new children being born are evidencing advanced mental and emotional capabilities that will probably be commonplace in all of humanity. I believe there will be widespread acceptance of spiritual intelligence which will include the recognition of past lives. I believe we will finally recognize nonphysical beings: angels and other celestial intelligences that are not embodied. In every culture on Earth there are stories of unusual experiences and enlightening contacts with beings that weren't physical.

Perhaps the 2012 alignment will lead us to a universal spirituality where deception and fear are no longer necessary. Perhaps our brand of manipulative politics will be replaced with a spiritual politics where every business will be environmentally and socially responsible. As Albert Einstein once said, "You can't solve a problem from the same level of consciousness that created the problem."

Our consciousness is the problem.

I Am Not Over
Caring About Time

Because I am an impatient person, and because I'm usually ten years ahead of the curve on many things, I have made a study of time in an effort to have more patience.

So far, Terry has been my most profound teacher where consciousness and time are concerned. She doesn't just relate to time in terms of when it's time to eat or go out. She has a sensitive calculator that is attached to her consciousness about other people's feelings. Once on a plane trip across country, she sat next to a woman with her paw on the woman's heart for five hours. At arrival, the woman told me that her daughter was dying and she was in a terrible state of depression. She said the energy from Terry's paw helped her.

I'm beginning to feel the "time of nature" now. I guess it takes ageing to do that. Living in New Mexico has helped to make me more patient. When I make an appointment for 2:00 on Tuesday, I'm learning not to get too upset when the person

I've hired shows up at 2:00 on Thursday instead. They are "on time," they say. There is a general deterioration in work ethic when time is money and *mañana* the rule of the day.

But sometimes when I'm involved in a project with other people and the sun is shining and the fish are jumping, I can't blame them for going fishing instead. There doesn't seem to be an acceleration of time or activity or much of anything in New Mexico.

Elsewhere is another story. People (particularly young people) are talking so fast, words tumbling over words, that they are impossible to understand. I am a stickler for enunciation, and I'll just stop them midsentence and tell them to go take some lessons in elocution and come back to tell me their story when they've learned how to care about whether they are being understood. The minds of people are going so fast their mouths can't keep up. This is a real problem with flight attendants on airplanes, assistants who answer phones for businesspeople, and machines that give you directions.

So I definitely feel the effect that the acceleration of time is having on human life. Terry keeps me grounded to the time of nature. I will take time to listen to the rustle of the leaves because her ears are perked up. Surrendering to her rhythm when we walk has helped me not to stumble. Watching her watch a bird in a tree has become hypnotic for me. She doesn't move a muscle, seems to even stop breathing. She becomes one with the bird and the tree and the moment. It is a moment of stop-time bliss.

But when I am stressed, I will stack items in my arms and fingers so I won't have to make another trip to another room. Of course I drop whatever it is and usually forget what I was so concerned about anyway. If I had to be patient and wait for a life or death verdict on something, I wouldn't know how to handle it. *God, give me patience and please do it now!*

So time is a subject that has raised my curiosity since I was young. I will attempt to simplify what I've read, and hope it is understandable. I'm not sure it is even to me.

I understand holographic time because of an out-of-body experience I had. I was in a boat on a river. You could say I was moving along a river of time. I knew what time it was immediately in front of me and immediately behind me, but as I was leaving my body I saw a far greater distance behind the boat on the river and a far greater distance up ahead. What time would that make each distance I was viewing? It was relative. I realized that all time was happening at once. If I had stayed on the boat the distance behind me would have been in the past. But viewing the scene from above I saw that I was seeing the past in the present. So, as Einstein promised, time is not linear. It is relative, which, as he says, means it doesn't really exist. We invented it so we could feel secure in what we call the present. Because of that experience I understand how our perception of time is relative. When it comes to my understanding space-time, it was more complicated.

When I relax and feel into time I realize that different times of the day and night have different qualities. It's as though time has various personalities. These various time qualities govern how we behave. Sunrise time affects us differently than midnight time. It's not just a question of the physical position of the sun and moon. It's also a question of when they are in space and that then becomes space-time. Every object in space-time is affected by the energy it encounters. So, since time doesn't stand still, neither does space. So no experience of space-time is the same as what went before. Therefore, boredom is impossible if a living being feels into the changing qualities of space-time.

To me, that is why live theater is so exciting and unnerving. It's never the same, not only because each audience is different, but because the space-time in which we perform is different. That is probably why so many people have stage fright. They can't rely on what they think they already know. I'm always fascinated when I perform live that it feels so entirely different every "time."

We live performers always wish we could capture what exquisite communication went on the night before. But that's impossible because everything in the personality quality of space-time is different, even an hour later. So I have come to understand that the Great Cosmic Clock in the sky is moving. Time moves and the clock moves. The changes in the quality of time concerns how we living beings are influenced. All of it is changing.

When I was in Peru doing *Out on a Limb,* the Peruvian

shamans told me that a new species of Homo sapiens was about to appear. They called the new humans "homo luminous." They told me that the forerunners of homo luminous were already among us. A new human was emerging, one that would possess qualities that we do not now have. That is because the qualities of space-time have not been as advanced before. They said our spiritual existence is a unique combination of free will and predestination. We each came in with a destiny, but free will can pull us out of alignment with that destiny. That is why it is so necessary to be in touch with our true selves. The true self is totally in touch with the movements of space-time and never fixed in either time or space.

From the ancient Egyptians to the Incas and Mayans, the Tibetans and the Hebrew kabbalists, they understood the secrets of the alchemy of time. In our modern times of stress and technology, we are diverting ourselves from these understandings. Therefore, we are out of sync with nature, time, and even our own destinies. The alchemists of Egypt and medieval Europe knew that time moved in great elongated cycles and that each part of each cycle had a precise quality. Those qualities shaped and reformed the world. When the cycles of time change, so do the events on Earth.

The sacred scientists and alchemists of our past used their perceptions of space-time to predict the future. Nostradamus somehow understood the mysterious process of space-time. He saw the different qualities of space-time in relation to the personalities of the people. And all of the mystics knew that their processes were tied to the precession of the equinoxes. They understood that the stars in the night sky were not fixed. Creating the zodiac system to assist them in their measurements of time, they used the twelve zodiac signs as a giant clock. They realized that it took 2,160 years to move through each sign of the zodiac, and it took nearly 26,000 years for the equinoxes to move through all twelve signs. The creation of the Great Year of 26,000 years gave them a clock that allowed them to measure time.

Then they came to understand that each of the signs (or places on the clock) appeared to bring forth changes in the quality of life here on Earth. The changes on Earth reflected the quality of each sign. And each 2,160 years, the quality of time changed.

So as I look at what I learned, I realize that we are coming to the end of the space-time that has been involved in the great 26,000-year cycle. The changes in the qualities of time cannot be held at bay. We are coming to the end of time as we knew it to be. We are in 2012 starting a new cycle of consciousness.

I feel it every day. For example, even as I write this I feel I am coming down with a cold or the flu. I increased my vitamins, I drink a lot of water, and I rest. But last night I had a dream about the intricacies of how to further avoid the real onset of the flu. I realized I had had the exact same dream a year ago when flu season came around. In the dream I remembered every detail of how to avoid getting really sick.

I never got the flu the year before, and I knew I wouldn't this year as long as I remembered the dream. What struck me, though, was that my brain had memory of the year-before dream stored. That meant that everything we think or experience is stored somewhere. It was the first time I realized what the Akashic Records meant.

Will We Ever Get Over the Akashic Records?

The universe itself has memory. It records and remembers everything that ever happened and is equipped with a dimension of consciousness that stores these memories, a dimension that is sometimes called the Akashic Records. Akasha is a Sanskrit word meaning "primarily substance, that out of which all things are formed." It is the crystallization of spirit. It is so sensitive that the slightest vibration anywhere in the universe (any thought or action) registers an indelible impression upon it. In modern terms it is the Book of Life.

Since each of us has a soul and a vibrational frequency, our thoughts and actions are equipped to be recorded in the Akashic Records, and those records can be accessed any time if we know how. Past-life therapy sessions enable us to access our Akashic Records. But the privacy of the Akashic Records of others is protected by veils of separation so they can't be used for any reason. When an adept or spiritual master has reached the level of universal trust, it is possible to read the records of others. A psychic is allowed to read the Akashic Records of a client because the energy and frequency of the client permits it. When we open the Akashic Records for our own perusal, we enter a mind state of universal oneness with the Divine.

I have felt this state when I do my past life therapy sessions. I'm never judgmental of myself or anyone else who has figured in my past when I touch the Records. I'm in a divine illumination which enables me to understand more clearly what my life has been about. My purpose becomes clear as has the road to understanding it. When I'm touching that divine knowledge, I am in a universal state of consciousness. I've found that the knowledge of who I am and who I have been is given to me at a manageable rate. It may be overwhelming at first, but is then met with a sense of relief. "Oh, that is what that was all about."

I'm told by the Dalai Lama that the Records are governed and protected by a group of nonphysical light beings called the Lords of the Records. When we access them, we are able to see the events and lessons of past incarnations. So the Akashic Records are the soul-level blueprint and the catalogue of experiences of an individual soul as it becomes aware of his or her spiritual journey through time.

The damage done by the Christian churches in eliminating the knowledge of the primary experience of a soul's journey through time is immeasurable. When we realize we have lived before and will live again, it instills in us a sense of cosmic justice that makes us responsible for our actions. When we believe that when we die there is no more, it gives us permission to express the worst in ourselves with no understanding of responsibility for our actions. It took Einstein and other scientists to prove that energy returns to its source. What one puts out, one gets back. Thus the laws of karma are obvious in scientific circles. Science understands and has proven that no energy ever dies—it just changes form.

So the idea that we only live one life is more detrimental than we can imagine. It can justify war, greed, and totalitarian control. But when we understand that what we do in this lifetime will dictate what needs to be cleaned up in the next, human behavior becomes more balanced and sane.

I so admire the behavior of the Dalai Lama in his relations with China. He has pointed out to the Tibetan people that in past incarnations they were cruel to the Chinese people for various geopolitical reasons and are now suffering some of that return energy.

I spent two weeks with the Dalai Lama in Brazil during the eco-conference in 1992. I learned a great deal about kindness, patience (not enough, some would say), and humor. It was fascinating to me that so many world leaders were unconsciously afraid of him. They seemed to innately understand that his system of cosmic justice was observing them. The absence of judgment on his part bothered them more than anything. I marveled at how the Dalai Lama stood in front of twenty thousand people and spoke without notes for hours. It was as though he was channeling some divine information (which I believe he was) to people who longed to understand but were not prepared to integrate it into their belief systems.

Sometimes, seemingly for no reason, he would stop talking and just laugh. He would laugh for minutes at a time as though watching a divine comedy in his head. He seemed to be a simple man, as we ate together, sat together, and traveled together. I have pictures of him that smile down on me from my Wall of Life. He lights up the room as though the pictures are alive.

I find it fascinating that his beliefs in the soul's journey through time (reincarnation) never elicit cynicism or derision, but that same belief from a Westerner who works in show business elicits derisive smirks. Maybe it's only a matter of wardrobe.

The Dalai Lama probably has less information in his Akashic Records than any other human because he chooses to keep coming back as what he was before. I've watched a ceremony where a new Panchen Lama was found because the child knew objects and information from the past. Perhaps this is the way the Buddhists help to maintain a fairly karmic-free individual because he is short on experience.

The Akashic Records are proof to me that all time is occurring at once. Because when they are accessed, they are not linear. And there is Akashic information about the probabilities in the future for each soul, depending on their free will.

All souls exist in perfection as part of the light of the Creator. With physical incarnational experience we accumulate karma. Our soul's decision to enact our free will and become physical is what is called third-dimensional life.

I remember one of my first physical incarnational experiences. I, as a cocreating soul with the God Creator, had fashioned a beautiful, gigantic, feather-winged lizard. I remember the iridescent colors of the feathers and the power of its body, which I wanted to fly with. I became so enamored with what I created that I entered its body and commanded it to fly. The experience was so exhilarating I didn't want to leave and float back to my home, the ethereal. As a soul, I desired to *live in the body of what I had created,* hence my first incarnational experience. After a while I had the feeling of being trapped. I knew my real soul-home was the nonphysical ether, but I couldn't get back. Such is the free will of creativity.

I remembered many other physical experiences determined by my free will creativity when I accessed my Akashic Records. The Records enable us to interact with our spiritual resource and gain insight and guidance and understanding of what we are doing with Earth time and space. This is why I've always been so interested in mystics and people who seem to operate with another reality, which I know is as real as that which is accepted. That was why I traveled so much and tried to learn about other cultures and points of view.

As I am ageing now, I am more interested in traveling within. It is a never-ending journey full of different time zones and physical color. I moved to New Mexico because it is close to the ancient shamanistic traditions of understanding other dimensional realities. When I visit Chaco Canyon, I enter the realm of my own Akashic Records and know that I lived there long ago. This has happened to me all over the world, from Peru to Russia, to China, to Israel, and elsewhere. I believe I have lived in each country I have traveled to. In fact, the purpose of my travels was probably to go home for a while.

My interest in the unseen realities of life is an act of going home too. That is why I never get bored. Life itself is what lies within. Each one of our times this time around has a vibrational frequency to it. So when we attempt to access the Records we need to say our name—or the name we go by. It's like having a cosmic internet of information where each one of us can access information.

This is how I do it.

I sit quietly in a chair with my bare feet planted on the ground or the floor. I make sure nothing is crossed, not arms, not legs, nothing. I sit up with a straight back and think of *nothing*. In this world it is easier said than done. If I say my name softly to myself and in my mind's eye over and over, I soon can achieve a kind of nothingness. Then I ask my Higher Self to access my Records for me in relation to the question I want an answer to. The Records usually only give me answers to my questions, nothing more.

Sometimes I get past, present, and even future answers because the Records encompass all three and even more. There are future possibilities in the answers, as well as probabilities and even eventualities. You can use your Records for all kinds of purposes: family matters, business growth, creative ideas in art and music, and of course, problem solving with another person. There are some simple rules to observe to get better results.

Don't begin a question with "when" because time as we know it does not exist in the Records. The Records are not bound by Earth time or space. So when you ask when will you get married and have children, the answer would probably be "when you find love" or something like that, unrelated to when.

It is best not to ask yes or no questions. They also are too limiting. The best questions are those that revolve around what, why, or how. It is not possible for negative or dark forces to influence the answers because all of the answers are protected by light, as are the Record Keepers, in order to preserve the integrity and purity of the Records.

I always *hear* the answers because I am more clairaudient than clairvoyant. I can be involved with any kind of activity (even driving along the freeway) and ask a question that I will receive an answer about. Sometimes what I hear is funny, sometimes quite serious, and oftentimes I think I'm hearing myself talk back to me. It stands to reason that the voice I hear is like my own because the information is being filtered through my Higher Self.

When my father was dying in the hospital, my Higher Self voice once said, "Take off his arm tourniquet, the nurse forgot to." My father couldn't speak and when I looked under the arm of his hospital robe, his skin had turned blue and he was in pain. When I removed it, he smiled so gratefully.

Often I ask my Higher Self which way to go in a traffic jam. It's always the correct answer and I save time (which doesn't exist anyway, so what was the point?). Still, even the most enlightened of us doesn't really want to sit in traffic!

I don't see energy fields and the like, I feel them. When I meet new people I sense them in a way that tells me I do or don't want to be around them. And when my friends ask me to comment on something going on in their lives, I fall into a kind of connected trance and usually whatever I say makes sense. At this stage of my life I'm so happy and at peace living alone so that I can explore the "inner otherness" of what it means to be alive.

When I meditate on the reality that the Akashic Records include *all life in the universe,* it is mind blasting. They are not just records of human energy, but of energies from all over the cosmos.

When I think about the alignment of 2012, is it possible that all the negative galactic energies down through 26,000 years will be transformed and erased? In other words, will the karmic laws of cause and effect no longer be there? Will we simply start incurring new karma with a more enlightened consciousness as we move into the new age of the Great Cycle?

I'm sorry that movies depict 2012 as a monumental disastrous event in order to rake in the money. We humans are so propagandized to be afraid that we actually pay money to feel it. The heads of networks and studios have told me that the *fear*-inducing films are so popular because people are so afraid in their own lives they look for fictional things to fear. It's safer. Fear is a fictionalized feeling anyway. It seems real but the reasons for fear can be reasoned away, particularly if we understand there is no death. Roosevelt said it best: "The only thing we have to fear is fear itself."

Entire civilizations are ruled by fear. I think so often of the piece of intelligence that came out of World War II. It was called Project Paperclip. It projected that the human race could be ruled by the fear of four things in the future, in the following order: First, fear of communism; second, fear of terrorism; third, fear of asteroids; fourth, fear of extraterrestrials.

We seem to be on schedule.

Fear of asteroids will probably take first place relating to the 2012 alignment, and soon after that will be the extraterrestrials who I believe basically only want to help us. That will be one for the Book. The Book of Life—the Akashic Records.

I Can't Get Over
My Frustration at Not Being
Able to Open Anything I Buy

I've broken every nail and nearly two fingers attempting to open sets of kitchen knives, sealed bottles, spices, makeup, vitamins, perfume, dog food, toothbrushes, hair brushes, and lipstick brushes. I'd like to brush up against the plastic-covering company's president and plaster him with a piece of my mind, which I'll probably break next, trying to open a hermetically sealed bottle of juice that could go bad because I can't get to it!

I Don't Want to Get Over the World Leaders I Have Met

One of the most impressive world leaders I have met is Ariel Sharon. Everyone called him Arik. I was in Israel with some friends, looking into the mysteries of the Old Testament and wondering about Armageddon.

I visited Arik in his office many times and he was always taking meetings and reading poetry at the same time. I sat beside him as his glass of tea dribbled down his shirt and crumbs of his Danish hit the floor. He was at once an everyman and quite a commanding spectacle, and he knew it. He waded through space when he walked and was a commander of all he surveyed.

Arik invited me to his ranch in the Negev Desert, where he baked bread for me under the stars. His wife was there, along with friends, as he performed this hospitality for me. He had named all of his animals and his plants, which he tended himself. He spoke of the beauty of the stars quite eloquently but never seemed to wonder what secret they might hold. He was an Old Testament warrior but never spoke of Armageddon. I noticed underneath a shock of hair on his forehead there were facial lines that formed a cross. When I brought that up, he quickly covered the lines with his hair. He knew how interested I was in metaphysics and the hidden codes of the Torah, from which the Bible Code had come later. He put on such a show for me, which I duly applauded and appreciated. He was profound, funny, yet extremely conservative, which was why he was endearing himself to me. Most of all, to me he was the most human of all the Israeli leaders I met. He knew I was an American liberal and he knew that I knew he was putting on a show for me. I only wished he would go deeper under the surface.

A year later I was playing the Gershwin Theater in New York. When the curtain came down and I was on my way to my dressing room, the stage door elevator opened and out waded Arik. "You were wonderful," he said. "Thank you." I was flabbergasted. No one even knew he was in New York, much less at the theater. We talked for a while. He hugged me and left with invisible Mossad guards protecting him.

My friend Bella Abzug had witnessed the embrace. She was sitting in my dressing room and was livid. "You are anti-Semitic," she said. "How could you consort with such a warmonger?"

I was genuinely shocked. Liking a conservative Jew made me anti-Semitic? She really meant it, too. She was my favorite friend but we had our differences. She attended many of my seminars as the "loyal opposition" and asked the harshest and most cynical questions. In fact once during a channeling session she was so "intellectually disturbed" by what was going on that she picked a fight with the spiritual guide coming through. She literally emptied the room. Yes, she had power even over spirit.

But Sharon was the Old Testament guardian of the supposed End Times. That was why he was so conservative. He and the American fundamentalist preachers agreed on most everything. I was too liberal to agree with their violent end-times prophecies.

Another impressive leader I met was Mikhail Gorbachev. He reminded me of my father, even the hairline. Whenever we've been together at meetings and conclaves he seems as though he looks right through me. I'd love to know what he was really thinking. He knows I know Roald Sagdaev, head of the Russian Space Agency, and maybe he's wondering what Sagdaev and I have talked about. Gorbachev is friendly but quite stern. I don't think he knows how to have fun. But I know he likes movie stars. I never met Raisa, his wife, but he has told me he wants a movie done on her life and he wants me to play her. I don't know how I feel about that. She, from what I know, would not be one of my favorite people. But it might be fun to play a character I don't like.

• • •

A female world leader who impressed me was Deng Yingchao, whom I met when I took a women's delegation to China. It was arranged by Chiao Kuan-hua, the head of the Chinese delegation in New York, and the sister of the Shah of Iran, Princess Ashraf. I had spent many nights at dinner in the Iranian Embassy in New York. The Iranians loved movie stars and hearing the latest gossip. Ambassador Hoveyda was my favorite of the group, and he was a film critic as well, who was published in Paris. I found myself at dinner one night at the Iranian Embassy with the Communist Chinese and the Imperialist Persians. Princess Ashraf was seated across from me, wearing a diamond around her neck that would have roused Richard Burton from the dead. As she leaned over to eat, her diamond came loose from its chain and landed in the rice pilaf. I quickly looked at her face. There was no expression. Very surreptitiously she retrieved the diamond from her plate, wiped it off with her napkin, and clipped it onto the chain again. No one knew any better except the white-gloved servant who stood with his tray of food, which was partly on fire because it was a special Persian hot entrée. His face betrayed no knowledge of what happened either. But Ashraf saw me see it, and pretty soon I had an invitation to go to China.

After Ashraf and the Shah were overthrown and Khomeini came in with the Revolution, I was horrified to see that

Hoveyda was one of the first persons put to death by being burned in an oven. Such is the drama of leadership and loss of life in this world.

When I mounted my delegation of women and went to China, one of the first people to greet us was Deng Yingchao, the wife of Chou En-lai. We were at a dancing event as she approached and I didn't know who she was. She was so unassuming and friendly. She introduced herself and we sat and talked with a translator. She shook hands with all the women in my delegation, and then we spoke together of the need for women all over the world to hold up the Other Half of the Sky. As we spoke woman to woman, I noticed that everyone had tears in their eyes, including Deng Yingchao. Soon her tears slid down her cheeks and she excused herself. I wondered what the Chinese Revolution had been like for her. And now their new revolution was the emancipation and power inclusion of women. I remembered my first reaction to the unisex wardrobe of the women in China. I felt that it was liberating and women as sex objects had become a thing of the past. Deng kept tabs on our adventures in China, and as we were leaving, she sent me a note to help support the other half of the sky in my country. I felt I had glimpsed a little bit beneath the surface of this communist woman.

I had met Indira Gandhi's father, Jawaharlal Nehru, when I was in India and then shared a plane ride with him on my way back home to New York. One thing about being a movie star is that most people want to meet you. So he had asked for me to sit with him on his visit to the U.N. (the year that Khrushchev banged his shoe on his desk). As we hovered over New York waiting to land, Nehru looked down at the skyscrapers and the U.N. building and said, "I must keep the doors of my country open but careful that the winds don't knock me off my feet." I think he used that line somewhere later, but it was very effective when I heard it.

When I met Indira Gandhi, she was most curious whether I worked for the CIA because I traveled so much. The Indian papers were full of my adventure in Bhutan when I got caught in a coup d'état. She smiled when I told her how much I loved adventure and I couldn't be programmed to work for anybody under their rules anyway. We spoke about relations between China and India. Even back then it was a major concern. She said the Sikhs were commissioned to patrol the border for safety and if any blood was drawn it was compulsory for them to kill the adversary. That left little room for mistakes.

We spoke of my intuitions that I had lived in India in the past. I told her I somehow was familiar with streets and temples. She was not surprised and said all of us humans had probably lived everywhere because we were, after all, a human family. I was happy that she, a woman in a position of great leadership, could still find opportunities to reveal some of her inner self to me, a relative stranger. That's a case for more women leaders, I'd say.

• • •

Fidel Castro was the most curious of the world leaders I've met. I was in Cuba after the opening of *The Turning Point* at a film festival. He took me away from Herb Ross (the director) and Nora Kaye (his wife and famous ballerina). He directed me to his office, where he questioned me about life in America for six hours while the other members of our delegation waited in the hall! He wanted to know about the Kennedys (so did I), Minute Maid orange juice, skyscrapers to the heavens, and, of course, Hollywood. I had heard that before the revolution he had been an extra carrying a spear in Cecil B. DeMille's extravaganza *The Ten Commandments*. He wondered where I heard it, but didn't answer. He asked about Barbara Walters, who had told me he would spirit me off into the sugar cane fields and charm me. I told him that and he loved it.

He continually talked about *los niños* (the children) and what he wanted their future to be like. He was dedicated and energetic, but I thought he was rude to the rest of the delegation. He did not ask about the Mafia, even though he knew I knew Sam Giancana and the others through Sinatra. He talked and talked like he does in his speeches and finally said he would see me later. As I was leaving, I complimented him on his uniform. I didn't know what he meant by "later," until that evening the doorbell rang in my hotel room. I opened it, and there stood Fidel with a box of cigars in one hand and a glass case with a dove in it in the other. One of his uniforms was draped over his arm. He was alone.

I wanted to call Barbara Walters, but it was too late.

He said the cigars were for Jimmy Carter and Brzezinski, and the dove was for me because I was a dove of peace. I didn't know if he wanted me to change into the uniform. He talked and talked about artistic freedom that needs to support and help the revolution. The fact that his country was nearly completely literate made him very proud. He said he didn't understand why our leaders were so against him (he didn't mention assassination). He said he wanted peace between us and he knew I knew Jimmy Carter and asked if I would convey his feelings to the president. I said I would.

We sat in two chairs with a table between us. Nothing that Barbara had warned me about occurred. (That made me wonder about her.) After a few hours he thanked me for listening to him and again reminded me to give the cigars to the president and Brzezinski.

What happened when I returned to the mainland was fascinating. First of all, my Cuban housekeeper unpacked my suitcase, saw Fidel's uniform, and promptly quit. When I went to the White House, Carter was busy so I brought the cigars to Brzezinski. We were in his office when he looked at the gift wrapping and said, "You open these. There might be a bomb inside."

I said okay and proceeded to take off the wrapping. The second I lifted the lid, Jimmy Carter left the Oval Office. A buzzer went off, and I jumped back. Oh my God, I thought, Brzezinski was right. Then I realized what had happened. Brzezinski wouldn't have anything to do with accepting the cigars. Instead he said, "You tell your friend Castro that we will smoke one of his cigars when he gets every last troop out of Angola." He turned around and walked away. Hamilton Jordan came in and helped himself to the cigars, endearing himself to me always.

Before I went to Cuba, I had arranged to do a live TV show from the Riviera Hotel on Varadero Beach in Havana. The director, the cast, and even Lillian Carter had agreed to do a time step with me on the sand. It was all financed and, I thought, okayed by the network. I told Fidel about it and he more than graciously offered to help any way he could. But as soon as I returned, all the agreements were somehow off. I don't know who reneged, whether it was the Cubans or the Americans. I just knew it wasn't going to happen.

The same thing happened to me when I was in China. We shot a wonderful film including our delegation's adventures in China. I called it *The Other Half of the Sky*. It was really very good and got nominated for a documentary Academy Award. But I couldn't get anyone to release it. People loved it, and even though I offered it to them for very little, no one would touch it. Ten years later as I was rehearsing for an Oscar show with Jack Valenti, he took me aside.

"You have a right to know what happened to your Chinese documentary," he said. I didn't know what he meant.

"Our State Department, along with the Chinese, told me [he was head of the Motion Picture Association] that if that film was released in the States, both China and America would boycott each other's films for ten years. I thought you should know the truth."

"Why did they do that?" I asked.

"Because in your film the women told the truth as they saw it. No government really likes that."

I was learning where the real power lay, no matter how attractive Hollywood was.

In politics, no matter what country you are in, everything is murky, coded, obfuscated. One South American leader, however, is the exception to that. My talks with President Menem of Argentina gave me hope about revealing the truth no one wanted to face. He wanted to talk to me about UFOs. He had read my books and was very personally interested in whether they were real or not. He said he had commissioned part of his military to keep a lookout and not to discredit anyone who said they had seen such things. He himself had seen what he thought was a UFO, but how could we really be sure?

We had long talks about their possible presence and why they were here. He knew that Jimmy Carter had written about them when he was governor of Georgia, and he knew the president of Mexico was inundated with inquiries because so many craft had been seen and photographed over Mexico, particularly Mt. Popocatepetl. He wanted to know what I thought and had I met with any of them. I told him that Carter knew they were here but couldn't get his intelligence people to confirm it. The NSA, CIA, and the military held the position that they were the permanent government, and that he, the president, was there only for a limited amount of time.

Menem was not at all concerned about the religious aspects of the presence of UFOs. The Catholic church had basically acknowledged "fellow beings in the universe" and was not opposed to making this public. But Carter was concerned as to what they were teaching. I told him that they were teaching the laws of physical reembodiment and we shouldn't be afraid of death. Carter then said, "Are they talking about reincarnation?" I said yes, and he said, "I'm a born-again Christian. I don't believe in any of that stuff."

That was basically the end of the investigative discussion and I have not broached the subject with him since, whenever we are together socially. Menem, on the other hand, was more interested in the truth than his religious convictions. The question of human religions is going to be a difficult one if and when the star beings show themselves with certainty.

I found the world leaders I met to be mostly politically motivated, but usually certain they were doing the right things for their people. I did say to myself quite often: would a woman leader behave like this? I knew a little about Golda Meir from those who knew and respected her. Gandhi carried on the leadership of her father, Nehru. I did not know Margaret Thatcher, nor did I want to. (I would have been afraid I'd break her hair.)

But I've wondered so often, in the loneliness of the dead of night, what would a woman leader really feel about sending young people off to war, and would she greet a star visitor with an attitude of welcome to help us out of the mess we've made of the planet?

Leaders I Will Never
Get Over (Personally)

Throughout much of my life, my attraction to certain men revolved around what unrealized talent *they* might have. If I found an exceptionally talented and intelligent man who hadn't yet been acknowledged, I would dig deep into his subconscious in order to find out why. Brilliant and talented (but unrealized) men became my specialty and my chosen endeavor. Even if I found a political leader attractive, I would intuit what he hadn't yet found himself capable of achieving.

When I met Olof Palme (the prime minister of Sweden), he was emotional catnip for me because he was such a liberal, brilliant, yet emotionally repressed Swede. I loved his courage on behalf of all his liberal beliefs. I met him at a U.N. anti–Vietnam War meeting in New York. He spoke so succinctly about the need to abolish war. He even spoke passionately about Democratic Socialism.

I remember the moment I fell for him. We were in my

New York apartment after the U.N. meeting. He was looking at the pictures on my New York Wall of Life. He smiled and I brushed the hair out of his eyes. He looked at my lips shyly, and I took him in my arms. That was it. We became lovers for years. We met in the Orient several times, and wherever his overseas goodwill trips took him. I took clandestine trips to Sweden and we kept the relationship private even though the Swedish press began to speculate why I was making so many private sojourns to Stockholm. He confided in me his struggles with some of the other world leaders and wondered aloud how the planet's inhabitants were ever going to solve its problems.

I introduced him to some of my beliefs regarding reincarnation and the soul's journey through time. He pooh-poohed all of it but did become interested in whether UFOs and star visitors were a reality we should admit to and deal with. His intellectual persuasion was definitely left-brained and scientific. Being a socialist meant more to him than anything. He was unreligious and bristled at the thought of an all-loving God-Creator. He thought it was all the work of humans and how we comported ourselves. He could be cruelly dismissive toward my growing spiritual beliefs and studies, but I admired his intellect greatly and thought seriously about a union of some kind with him. He was technically married but had had other affairs aside from me. One of his women was an extremely wealthy communist and I found the contradiction intriguing. In hindsight, I wonder if his attraction to fame and money was more true to his personality than his professed attraction to socialism.

Through my relationship with Palme I learned that the leaders in the world who were Democratic Socialists formed a kind of fraternity with each other. They knew each other's habits and preferences. Later, when I had a short fling with Pierre Trudeau, he knew about my relationship with Palme. All of the Democratic Socialists were heavily involved in the machinations of the U.N. They were "citizens of the world," which I found attractive. It appealed to my global liberalism and fit in with my belief in travel as the best source of true education.

Palme had been easygoing and flexible in our personal relationship; Trudeau was autocratic and dictatorial. Once when Pierre visited me in LA he wanted to see a movie studio. I drove us up to the gate on the Fox lot. Even though the guard recognized me and paid his respects to the prime minister of Canada, he said he couldn't let us through because no one had given him permission. I'll never forget Pierre looking longingly at the New York street set from *Hello Dolly,* the house from *The Sound of Music* visible in the background, as he was told he wasn't allowed in. He may have been above it all in his political life, but when it came to the Dream Factory, he was as wide-eyed and eager as anyone else.

Pierre was conversant with spiritual science, probably because he had had an education in the French Charismatic Catholic point of view. Miracles were part of his faith and his world view. Charismatic Catholics have no problem with metaphysics (that is, things beyond the physical). I noticed that when I'd do press conferences in Paris to promote a movie, the French press wanted to talk about my books. I enjoyed the French intellectual questions very much regardless of how insufferable they could sometimes be.

I liked playing my live show in Paris too. The audiences understood the deeper meaning of movement and lyrics and the well-thought-out dramatic harmony of the music I had put together. I never saw Yves Montand when I played Paris. But he did send me flowers with a card saying "from one legend to another."

My longest-lasting relationship with a political leader was with Andrew Peacock (foreign minister of Australia and Australian ambassador to the United States). I met him while I was playing in Australia (set up by a mutual friend from Princeton). He was charming, funny, and a conservative. He used his voice like a snake oil salesman, which always made me laugh because, as I told him, I was also in the business of professional seduction through voice manipulation. He took my comment good-naturedly.

Andrew and I traveled all over the world together, as the pictures on my walls attest. He was fun as a traveling companion, and his being a foreign minister opened many doors in high places. He didn't know about Palme and threatened to have his Secret Service follow me if I was ever caught with anyone else. Once after leaving Palme in Stockholm, I went directly to Paris to meet Andrew. The paparazzi were all over me when I landed. Andrew thought it was because of him, but it was actually about both Palme and him. The paparazzi must have thought I was Mata Hari or something. Andrew and I eluded them by ducking into strange doorways, darting down unknown alleys, and once climbing up the side of a building to get away. Andrew's image would have been blown had the pictures of our mad dash reached the newspapers, because he had cultivated the image of being blue-blood elegant through and through. He was single, so I told the press I was going to give him a foreign affair he'd never forget.

We traveled in Canada, France, Cambodia, Thailand, Australia, England, the United States, and Mexico. Whenever I discussed my spiritual and metaphysical ideas with him, he listened, nodded, and more or less said, "It could be. Who knows?" On a UFO stakeout in Mexico near Mt. Popocatepetl, at one moment we thought we saw a craft and Andrew nearly "climbed the sky" to see if it was real.

As foreign minister he controlled all the information coming out of Alice Springs (supposedly the underground UFO research facility in Australia). Because he was sworn to secrecy, he never told me outright that UFOs were extraterrestrial in origin and were present. But he said and did nothing to disabuse me of such a belief. When I told him about Roald Sagdaev having confirmed that UFOs and the presence of ETs were real, he just smiled. When I told him I had gone to see Jimmy Carter to discuss UFOs, he just smiled again. Andrew was a trained diplomat of the first order and was his own best intelligence gatherer. He was learning more about the subject of UFOs from me than I was learning from him.

We have been friends for over thirty years, and we value each other very much. He is happily married now for the third time, and I remain friends with his children and his first wife, too.

When I look back on my relationships with political men of power, I'm always astonished at how incidental they seem to me now. It was more about my need to touch power and influence than it was about the individuals. Is that how it really is with all of our accumulated relationships? At the time they are all-consuming, life-and-death experiences. But in the end it is actually all about us and what we needed or identified with. Because of my years of being politically active, I needed to understand what politicians actually went through. What kept them awake at night? What motivated them to save the world or to destroy it?

Most interesting to me was the power that they abused in a sexual sense. Political power meant sexual power to them. They could have any woman they wanted. Everyone accepted the fact that if you occupied a position of leadership power, sexual promiscuity went along with it. It came with the territory. Their wives looked the other way, knowing the future would be different when they were all old and gray. I've known several political leaders who were ultrapromiscuous, yet later on when their wives died, they suffered from unspeakable sorrow and guilt. The thrill of the clandestine left them alone without companionship later in life. If they had known that, would they have done it again? Probably. Everyone does what they do in order to learn about themselves. Some are just slow learners.

Does Anyone Get Over Sex and Power?

Everyone knows that power is an aphrodisiac. I guess that was true for me too, except what I found sexy was the power to help people. To me, that was what leadership was all about. In fact, if I knew someone in power who *wasn't* doing his utmost to make things better, it was a surefire turnoff. Obviously, Hollywood people find political power sexy, and political power people find Hollywood sexy.

I never had any proof that the Kennedy brothers had intimate relations with Marilyn Monroe, but it wouldn't be beyond the realm of probability. Once at Arthur and Mathilde Krim's house in New York, I joined an impressive gathering of movie stars and politicians. Marilyn was there. I saw her go into a private room with Jack. They stayed awhile, until he came out another door. Immediately, Bobby entered the room and stayed until the song that Jimmy Durante was singing was over. I have a picture of that night on my Wall of Life. Of course, the Kennedy brothers and Marilyn could have been talking world affairs and comparing notes, but most of us thought it was the other kind of affairs they were interested in.

My own relationship with the Kennedys was what I'd call "sexually hilarious." Before he was president, Jack often drove me in his convertible when he visited Hollywood. He must have been remembering every film he ever saw. We'd drive to Mulholland Drive, look out over the lights of the city and the San Fernando Valley, and *talk*. He wanted to know about people and their political persuasions. He wanted to know about how pictures were made. He never made a pass at me or anything. In fact, I wondered what was wrong with me.

Being in Bobby's company was another story. Once during the Kennedy campaign, Bobby and his cohorts invited a bunch of us Hollywood types to spend a weekend in Palm Springs. I thought, why not? We all had a nice dinner at a huge table. Then we danced to the music of the day. It was amusing for me to see the future attorney general, the man who would go after the Mafia, doing the Twist for all he was worth. Some time after midnight we retired to our hotel rooms. My room was part of a huge suite that the Kennedy campaign had rented. I said goodnight to all the stragglers from the dance floor, showered, and got into bed.

When I was half asleep, my door opened and a man entered and climbed into bed with me. I didn't know who it was. I sat up and rolled over onto the floor. I was one of those people who had to know a little something about the person I was having sex with. The man climbed back out of bed and left. I got back into bed. Fifteen minutes later, another man came into the room and climbed in bed with me. I had no idea who he was either. Again, I rolled out of bed onto the floor.

This went on all night until I finally slept on the floor. I have no idea who the men were, or whether it was the same persistent man. When I got up the next morning, everyone was gone. Maybe that was the way the Kennedy crowd did sex—anonymously and with plausible deniability.

A political campaign arouses intense sexual power. I think everyone involved is so excited by their daily illusions of moving around the furniture in the White House that they need to express that illusionary power through sex. Also, it is accepted. It's like being on location when making a movie. No commitment is necessary and everyone is in it together—literally.

I am basically a serial monogamist. One man at a time until the relationship is over. But once during a campaign (and I was involved with many), I decided I would be daring like everyone else. I had sex with three men in one day. It was stupid and brought me no satisfaction. At the end of that day, someone set the campaign headquarters on fire. It certainly wasn't me.

It's puzzling what illusions of grandeur do to the sex drive. There is a compulsion to be joined with another person. I wonder what the seven chakras look like all lit up during a campaign! No one sleeps, no one really eats, and no one feels responsible for their own personal behavior because everyone feels they are contributing to something bigger, above and beyond themselves. The candidate usually needs to feel he is tending to his loyal flock by propagating his masculine prowess. And the flock feels it needs to reflect the candidate's ability to be in charge by submitting to him. There's also a subliminal message that you are not really part of the flock if you abstain. The shock of reality comes after you win or lose. If you win, then it's a competition for acknowledgment (appointed positions, etc.). If you lose, you just go home to lick your wounds and hope you are welcomed back to the place you came from.

Another reason sexual expression may be intense during a campaign is that every individual involved is living with a sense of him- or herself as being dedicated to a higher cause. You believe in the candidate and what he stands for. You believe you can change the world. You believe you have a kind of power you never felt before. I guess that translates in a physical way into SEX and release.

The press corps covering the campaign always lurks, always watches, and sometimes, whether invited to or not, gets in on the action. We've all heard stories, particularly relating to the Kennedys, but for both the watchers and the watchees to be part of the same action must play havoc with how they do their jobs. The "people out there" wouldn't approve, although all of them would participate unless they were intimidated by what they secretly crave: sex and glamour and power. So the journalists and the glamorous campaigns they cover are doing one thing and speaking another. That's when you understand that sex is the great motivator for hypocrisy. I've never understood why. Why is it such a subject for annihilation of character? Why doesn't that fall to murder, greed, lying, and cheating? Why does anyone care about what somebody else does with his or her sexuality?

I Am Not Over the Founding Fathers

The intensity of my feelings about the birth of America was explained when I allowed myself to believe that I had been there when it happened. It also explains my spiritual leanings and my political activism in regard to what I believe this country stands for.

Many books have been written about the people who were part of our Constitutional Convention, and the information they reveal feels very familiar to me. Two books, one by Walter Jenkins and another by Walter Semkiw, did a study of the past lives of famous people and they specifically revealed what they believe was one of my past identities. Neither author knew the other. They both claimed through channeled sources that I was Robert Morris. Robert Morris has been called the forgotten patriot because he underwrote a great part of the Revolution and yet died penniless in a pauper's prison. Potentially being a *man* in the American Revolution was not surprising to me. I knew I hadn't been sewing flags.

And I have always had a strange fear of being penniless and imprisoned. I didn't know where that came from. It's possible that now I do know. There are many other similarities. Morris possessed psychic gifts that I have, too, if I allow myself to remain open. Morris shared a love of philosophy and investigation of metaphysics with his father, just as I have. Morris was good with money, as I am, until he spent it all on the Revolution. Morris moved on the spur of the moment. He never liked to plan. Neither do I, much to the consternation of my family and friends.

He was extremely punctual, as I am, and I am very judgmental of people who are late (as I've said, New Mexico is a good test of patience for me). Morris loved the sea. I have lived by the Pacific (in Malibu) ever since I left the East Coast. I keep a place there still. One of the reasons I moved to New Mexico is because I sense the Pacific coast will be inundated by a tsunami. I don't know when. But it will happen as a result of an undersea earthquake.

Morris was an inveterate traveler, as I have been. He built his house on a mountaintop. So have I. There was a touch of P. T. Barnum in Morris. That is surely true of me. He was very curious about China and sent a ship there to explore trading possibilities. I formed a delegation to go with me to China. But most of all, I am dedicated to the American Constitution. Morris was an important delegate to the Constitutional Convention.

In one of my books I wrote: "The men who signed the

Bill of Rights and drew up the Constitution said they wanted
to form a new republic based on spiritual values. And those
values they believed in went all the way back to the beliefs of
Hindu scriptures and Egyptian mysticism. That's why they
put the pyramid on the dollar bill—in fact the dollar bill and
the Great Seal are full of spiritual symbols that link way back
to long before the revolution, and all those pre-Christian beliefs had to do with reincarnation. . . ."

I mention this because many of our Founding Fathers were
transcendentalists and 33rd Degree Masons. They were our
original politicians, yet none of the people in politics these
days seem to know the origins of our democracy. They spoke
of having a vision of enlightenment for the new nation. They
fashioned the Great Seal out of sacred geometry because they
were Masons. The city of Washington was modeled along
sacred geometric lines. We have metaphysical roots underpin-
ning our national identity.

Freemasons, at the most basic level, believed in the fun-
damental metaphysics of the Enlightenment. They believed
that cosmic truths could be applied to creating harmony in
a new society. They believed people could be self-governing
and self-correcting. They warned against being ignorant of
ignorance. They cautioned us against losing the foundations
of our spiritual identity.

The Masonic sacred geometry we see in physical form in
Washington, D.C., and in the great cathedrals of Europe
dates back to Solomon's temple. Sacred geometry is based on

the harmonics of space, sound, light, and the re-creation of the principles of the cosmos and nature, which are also duplicated in the human body and human consciousness.

The Founding Fathers believed that the ability to reason was defined as the ability to see the divine patterns which pre-exist in nature. On the Great Seal there is the eagle, which was known as the bird of Zeus (God). The bird stood for the in-carnational principle of the deity coming to the field of action (Earth) and into the field of opposites (war and peace). In one of the eagle's talons he holds thirteen arrows (war). In the other a laurel branch with thirteen leaves (peace). The eagle is looking in the direction of the laurel, indicating a desire for diplomatic solutions. Nine feathers are in the eagle's tail (nine is divine power descended to Earth). Over the eagle's head are thirteen stars arranged in the form of the Star of David or Solomon's Seal. They represent the Zodiac, including God, and the thirteen original colonies.

The Rainbow Body of the Iroquois (seven colors represent-ing seven chakras) signified the complexity of long life but a prophecy of peace. The Founding Fathers felt a chromatic link between music and the rainbow and the scales of sound and color. They said the Creator instilled that harmony in each of us, that these truths were self-evident. Much of our Constitution was based on the Iroquois Nation's system of self-governing and self-correcting. As above, so below. The astrological Zodiac was self-governing and self-correcting.

I have been working on understanding these principles

since I was a very young girl and will continue to do so until I transition into what comes next. When I visited Monticello, I made friends with the curator and he let me sleep overnight in Jefferson's bedroom. There was thunder and lightning that night. I sat very still in the center of the banquette trying to feel Jefferson. I couldn't remember the relationship I'd had with him, when (and if) I was his contemporary, Robert Morris. There were copies of his Jeffersonian Bible on a table. I sat reading his denunciation of religion, ducking each time the thunder and lightning roared outside the window. A pair of his glasses rested beside a candle. Just above his desk there was a loft where he and Sally Hemings sometimes slept. No one would have known they were sleeping in the cavelike loft. I didn't go in the loft. Too invasive, I thought.

In between lightning strikes I felt a presence. It was quiet, but commanding. Then I heard a whistle. I whirled around. Nothing there. Soon after, I fell asleep on the banquette. In the morning, the guards came in and gently woke me. One of them looked out the window, then back at me.

"Jefferson walked last night," he said. "He walked and whistled."

"How often does that happen?" I asked.

The guard smiled. "Every night. But last night he knew you were here."

I'll never forget my visit to Jefferson's home. The guard said he had loved it so much he never wanted to leave it. As I was preparing to go on my way, the curator handed me a small package. Enclosed was a glass case and inside was a single lock of Jefferson's hair. I still have it. The "authorities" knew I had it and wanted to check the DNA bloodline from it. But I wouldn't give it to them. As I waved goodbye, one of the guards waved goodbye and said, "We'll say hello to the great gentleman for you because he walks and whistles every night."

I'm sure I was there at the birth of our nation, and when I look at what has become of our original dream I simply can't fathom it. It's time we looked at how "self-evident" we've become.

I hope I don't end up penniless and in prison again for speaking out about how far off our transcendentalist track we've wandered.

It's Not Over Yet . . .

I am very happy in my life. I live alone with my Terry and my friends who come in and out of my beautiful home in Santa Fe. I teach seminars in spirituality and run a Spiritual Boot Camp at my ranch. I still work in films—when a good one comes along. I'm back on the stage, appearing in theaters around the country in an evening that is a mixture of show business, movie business, and Is-ness business (spirituality and metaphysics). It's all the same thing really. I have learned, profoundly, in my life that I create my own reality every minute of the day *and* night. I enjoy interacting with the live audience.

After so much searching and traveling, I can't get over the belief that the philosophic and spiritual cultures of ancient Greece, Egypt, and India were superior to our mechanistic, technological, and cynically skeptical culture of today.

We have forgotten the haunting truths of mysticism. The mystics were supposedly channeling the truths from the gods.

Much of what they taught contributes now to the divine secrets of the sciences. Science is becoming freer to include the spiritual aspects of reality. It admits more and more that there is a spiritual ignorance we must get over, that we all must feel free of ridicule as we pursue truth. After all, science exists mainly to explain God and reality.

But there is so much to get over in pursuit of our freedom of thought.

The memories of our lives as spiritual beings seem to have vanished from our objective minds as we focus predominantly upon making money with the political and commercial circus. So many people feel ignorant of their purpose in life, ignorant of what lies beyond the mystery of death, ignorant of why we are here. We know somehow that our souls are inextricably bound to the divine, but we can't seem to touch the connection. We are ignorant of our ignorance.

Intellectuals and hard evidence scientists have appointed themselves the final judges of all knowledge, both human and divine. Most of them believe that mystics are delusional and saints are religious neurotics. Most say God is a primitive superstition, that the universe is an accident with no particular harmony, that nothing exists after death, and certainly we don't live again.

People everywhere feel ground down by a soulless culture which heralds competition, money, and fame. They long for some kind of enlightenment and meaning within themselves.

They are sensing that commercial materialism is actually impractical, that there is some other truth that is more satisfying and long-lasting.

People who once felt perfectly content living in the material world, now confronted with its sinking economics, are seeking happiness elsewhere but don't know where to look. We sense that it lies within the soul's understanding, but we get no reinforcement for the search. From experience, I know that those who attempt such a search are often ridiculed.

Most modern scientists and academics regard thinking as a purely intellectual process. Yet the power to speculate in more feeling and intuitive ways will be the saving grace of humanity. I believe the supreme source of power is the unfolding of the spirit within each of us, the God-force within.

The ancient philosophers knew that living according to the power within superseded the intellectual powers. The power within was the yin. The intellectual power was the yang. We know that the entire universe is made up of yin and yang, masculine and feminine, thrust and receive, night and day. The balance of the two can be the foundation of the New Philosophy, the New Spirituality, the New Age.

No one can live in happiness without finding and articulating a spiritual philosophy for themselves. Neither can a nation. And that spiritual philosophy must dedicate its existence to advancing policies that are consistent with its core beliefs. That is what our Founding Fathers dedicated themselves to.

Our modern world makes a philosophy of its own fabrications. Its gods are of its own fashioning. We have forgotten how much we actually know. We believe that the physical reality is all there is. But an emphasis on our inner spirituality would lead us into a land of peace where the knowledge within would be given outer expression. Every blade of grass would be respected for its being. And its purpose would be self-evident to us. The yearning of humanity would find its wisdom in the soul of every living entity. The struggle from the womb to the tomb would have meaning and purpose and wisdom. The physical is not the true measure of truth.

The soul reaches out to the stars, knowing it is not alone, and our soul's spirit mingles with all there is in the cosmos. That is when we "feelingly" comprehend the wonders of the universe. What we didn't know was only what we were not conscious of.

We are reborn when we see what we are looking at. The barriers are down. All mysteries are returned to us as answers. They permeate everything within us. Then our reality changes. Through the spiritualization of our emotions we would see the real sadness of the human race and what it could be if we looked within *and* without ourselves with open hearts.

That has been my experience. I see the possibilities beyond the stars, possibilities that could unite us with our neighbors and with our own human potential if we would only acknowledge their existence. Free spirituality would release us from our materialistic bondage and from the restrictions of religion.

We would move into the light, into being transcendentalists, into manifesting that which our Founding Fathers dreamed. We, like nature and the mystics, would be self-governing in our connection to the Divine. *E pluribus unum.* Out of many comes one. A new order and a new age begin, and the deity, which is both male and female equally, is reflected in each of our higher selves.

Our own perfection is yet to be reached, but that is what gives us a purpose in being alive.

I will not get over this.